PITTSBURG STATE UNIVERSITY

PITTSBURG STATE UNIVERSITY

A Photographic History of the First 100 Years

RANDY ROBERTS &
SHANNON PHILLIPS

Foreword by Tom W. Bryant

University Press of Kansas

Artist Tom Corbin created the bronze statue *Student's Life,* which was installed in the
F. Victor Sullivan Courtyard at the Kansas Technology Center in April 2005.

Publication made possible by the Pittsburg State University Foundation, Inc.
Photographs courtesy of Pittsburg State University, Special Collections and University Archives

Published by the University Press of Kansas (Lawrence, Kansas 66045), which was organized by
the Kansas Board of Regents and is operated and funded by Emporia State University,
Fort Hays State University, Kansas State University, Pittsburg State University,
the University of Kansas, and Wichita State University.

Library of Congress Cataloging-in-Publication Data
Roberts, Randy.
Pittsburg State University : a photographic history of the first 100 years /
Randy Roberts and Shannon Phillips ; foreword by Tom W. Bryant.
p. cm.
Includes bibliographical references and index.
ISBN 978-0-7006-1644-2 (cloth : alk. paper)
1. Pittsburg State University—History. 2. Pittsburg State University—History—Pictorial works.
I. Phillips, Shannon. II. Title.
LD4561.P69R63 2009
378.748'86—dc22
2008045575

Printed in China
10 9 8 7 6 5 4 3 2 1

The paper used in this publication is acid free and meets the minimum requirements
of the American National Standard for Permanence of Paper for
Printed Library Materials z39.48-1992.

Contents

Foreword

A S YOU TURN THE PAGES of this book, you will see that the history of Pittsburg State University is a rich, colorful story that many people have had a hand in writing.

Some names come to mind immediately. People like William A. Brandenburg, R. S. Russ, Odella Nation, Harry Hartman, and others played pivotal roles in building and shaping the university. There were many, many others, however, whose names may not be so well known, but who also played a part in creating the university we know and love today.

One might even argue that every person who has worked at what today is Pittsburg State University, as well as every student who has studied here and all the citizens who have supported the university so faithfully over the years, can take some credit for creating and sustaining this modern, vital place of higher learning.

While we honor those who came before and we value greatly their contributions, we know that Pittsburg State University is more than a few personalities and more than an impressive collection of buildings. Most important, Pittsburg State University is a set of ideals—ideals that were set down when the first classes were held in 1903 and that guide the university still today. First among them is a belief in the ability of knowledge to transform the life of every person.

If William A. Brandenburg were to walk across the Oval today, he would see a place that looks much different from the institution he helped build. He would, however, recognize a place where students are still valued and where education continues to open doors and change lives.

A century from now, when others are writing the next chapter in Pittsburg State University's story, much will have changed. Technology, fashion, new buildings to accommodate growth—each will have its effect. More names will be added to history's list. Although much will change in the decades ahead, we hope and expect that the core values that have guided this university so well and have stood the test of time will remain and that Pittsburg State University will continue to be a place where knowledge changes lives and where aspirations are born.

I hope for each of you who read this pictorial presentation of the history of Pittsburg State University that you relive your experience with many fond memories of this fine university.

Dr. Tom W. Bryant
President

Acknowledgments

THE AUTHORS ARE GRATEFUL to Pittsburg State University President Tom Bryant for the opportunity to work on this fulfilling project and for his generous support and encouragement throughout. A special thank-you also goes to Mrs. Joan Cleland of the President's Office for all of her cheerful assistance.

The authors are also deeply indebted to Mr. Malcolm Turner, university photographer, for many of the best photographs included in this volume and for his technical assistance.

Finally, the generous assistance and encouragement of the editorial and production staff of the University Press of Kansas was greatly appreciated by the authors.

Chapter One

BEGINNINGS

No individual shall be obliged to choose between an education
without vocation, and a vocation without an education.

Russell S. Russ

A T THE TURN of the twentieth century, the city of Pittsburg, Kansas, was at a critical economic crossroads. Heavy industry had replaced sustenance farming as the region's dominant occupation. The effects of this change on the job market would have critical implications for area schools and would give birth to what has become Pittsburg State University.

On March 6, 1903, Governor Willis J. Bailey signed a bill that authorized the establishment of a school that would train teachers in the manual and domestic arts. Public schools faced an increasing demand for practical training that prepared youth not for college, but for the changing job market, and qualified teachers were not readily available. When this new school opened, it was called the Kansas State Manual Training Normal School Auxiliary—an auspicious name for an institution with a distinguished future. Since 1903 the university has forged proud traditions in academics, in athletics, and in service. This growth, and the recognition that went along with it, is traced through the institution's numerous name changes. With each name change came greater influence and opportunity. In 1923 the school achieved statewide recognition, becoming Kansas State Teachers College. By 1959 the

academic program had expanded so far beyond the teaching curriculum that it dropped the word "teachers" and became simply Kansas State College of Pittsburg. The most recent metamorphosis came in 1977, when the institution became Pittsburg State University.

Early groundwork for industrial and technical education began in the fall of 1897, when Russell S. Russ became superintendent of schools in Pittsburg. Within two years Russ had introduced a woodworking course into the Pittsburg high school curriculum—the first manual training course to be offered in the state. Courses in metalwork, cooking, and sewing soon followed. Russ correctly believed this hands-on, practical curriculum could reduce the number of students who dropped out of high school before graduation. The positive results attracted favorable attention from local residents and from surrounding communities. Superintendents and principals throughout the region, eager to reduce their own dropout numbers, sought Russ's advice and assistance to institute manual training courses in their schools.

The addition of manual training courses in Kansas schools created a demand for teachers qualified in the industrial and domestic fields. Russ envisioned the establishment of a school dedicated to preparing

Russell Station Russ, founder of the State Manual Training Normal in Pittsburg, served as the first principal of the school from 1903 to 1911. The Kansas Board of Regents fired Russ for his role in the struggle to separate Pittsburg from the State Normal School in Emporia. Ironically, Russ had graduated from the Normal School in Emporia with a lifetime teaching certificate in 1892. After his dismissal in 1911, Russ was never again a teacher, but he served briefly on the Pittsburg Board of Education and went on to have a successful career in the banking industry.

Ebenezer F. Porter moved to Pittsburg in 1890 to open a grain and lumber business. In 1900 he was elected to the state senate to represent Crawford County. During his second term he sponsored legislation that permitted all Kansas high schools to offer manual training and domestic courses. Porter anticipated that the State Normal School in Emporia would not expand its curriculum to include manual training coursework. He sponsored Senate Bill 234 to establish the Manual Training Normal School in Pittsburg. Crawford County Representative Fred B. Wheeler wrote to Pittsburg attorney Morris Cliggitt that behind-the-scenes politicking "had been so intense that Senator Porter was nearly in a state of physical and mental exhaustion, having come close to having a nervous breakdown."

teachers in these new curriculum areas, and he convinced State Senator Ebenezer F. Porter and other Pittsburg politicians to make such a school a reality. The legislature provided that the new school would be under the supervision of the Board of Regents and Jasper N. Wilkinson, president of the State Normal School in Emporia. Nine thousand dollars was appropriated for each of the first two years to begin the work. The Pittsburg Board of Education agreed to furnish the necessary school building.

There was widespread opposition to adding another school to the Kansas system of higher education. Opponents of Porter's proposed legislation believed Kansas operated quite well with an agricultural college in Manhattan, a liberal arts university in Lawrence, the teachers' normal school in Emporia, and the western branch of the Emporia normal established at Fort Hays in 1902. Newspapers quoted one

legislator as saying, "I am against this bill because it provides for a needless expenditure of good Kansas money. And what for? To build a school away down in an out-of-the way corner of the state where it will benefit no one but people from Missouri and Oklahoma." Another senator added, "Kansas can find a better place to spend money than in Crawford County. What is there in southeastern Kansas anyway? Nothing but Bad Lands, . . . and Pittsburg is nothing but a coal mining camp." In response, Senator Porter stated: "Pittsburg is in the center of a thriving industrial region and is already the seventh largest city in the state. In this day and age it is only logical to teach the practicalities of industry and homemaking as well."

The Central School Building, located on the northwest corner of Fifth and Walnut streets in Pittsburg, served as the first home of the State Manual Training Normal School Auxiliary. The Pittsburg Board of Education loaned the building to the normal. Central School was originally constructed to be a high school in 1893. A small blacksmith shop was erected on the school grounds as part of the normal school's operations and a vacant church building to the north was rented to serve as a library.

As E. A. Ross, president of the Kansas Board of Regents, told his hometown newspaper, the *Burr Oak Herald,* on May 7, 1903, "The little city of Pittsburg has a population of about 16,000 and the board of trade is composed of live men, wide awake to the needs of the town and thoroughly able to make their wants known. It is in the most populous portion of the state. It is a great industrial city. The manual training school was very properly located amid such surroundings and we confidently expect to see, in a very few years, a great educational institution built up at this place which will be a credit, not only to the city and state of Kansas, but the entire western country as well."

On September 8, 1903, the State Manual Training Normal opened with five faculty members and fifty-four enrolled students. The enrollment increased to seventy before the start of the second ten-week session. The students came from twenty-two Kansas counties; three communities in Missouri; La Salle, Illinois; Afton and Hawarden, Iowa; and Bartlesville and Tulsa in the Indian Territory of Oklahoma. Students were attracted to the school by advertisements that noted that tuition was free for Kansas residents. In addition, living expenses were as low as at any school in the state, students could enroll at any time of the year, and it was the only school in the state that prepared students to meet the requirements of the new manual training curriculum law, which mandated manual training courses in all the state's public schools. The enrollment at Pittsburg rose to 142 by June 1904, the first graduating class of ten students received their diplomas, and the prospects for the school's success seemed bright.

Josephine Shellabarger was the first instructor of domestic arts and sciences, from 1903 until she resigned in the summer of 1905. She graduated from Clark University in Worcester, Massachusetts, and completed additional credits at the University of Kansas. During the summer of 1903 she was offered a position at the University of Texas in Austin but decided to accept the appointment in Pittsburg following an interview with R. S. Russ. Soon after her resignation, Shellabarger married Pittsburg businessman Otto H. Greef and moved to Kansas City, Missouri.

The first college orchestra was established in 1905. Clayton Hale (holding cornet), a student from Girard, Kansas, took the initiative to organize the orchestra. Professor Edwin A. Shepardson (holding trombone), an original member of the faculty who taught English and history, volunteered his leadership. Shepardson became the first head of the Department of Mathematics when it was created in 1912 and held the position until resigning in 1915. Left to right: Isadora Arnold, Clayton Hale, Eva Eakin, Maud Gunn, Ethel Morrill, Don Gilbert, Edwin A. Shepardson, and Florence Byron.

Albert M. Bumann was a member of the original faculty and the first head of the Department of Manual Training. Bumann graduated from the St. Louis Manual Training School of Washington University in 1885, the first manual training high school in the United States. In 1911 Bumann drew the plans for the Industrial Arts Building, the second classroom building on the campus. In 1913 Bumann resigned to accept a similar appointment at the Northeast State Normal School in Tahlequah, Oklahoma.

Odella Nation was the first person the Board of Regents named to the original faculty. She held a teaching certificate from the State Normal School in Emporia and graduated from the Kansas City Business College in 1902. Nation taught business courses from 1903 to 1905, and she served as the private secretary to Principal R. S. Russ and financial secretary for the school from 1903 to 1911. She also served as head librarian from 1903 to 1943 and cataloging librarian from 1943 until her retirement in August 1951.

Sarah Preswick Chandler was the first student to enroll in the new Manual Training Normal School in Pittsburg. She was also among the first ten students who graduated in June 1904. In 1910 the school promoted Chandler from professor to director of domestic arts. Chandler lost her position in 1911 after the dismissal of R. S. Russ. She later married Robert Hartsock and lived the remainder of her life in Oklahoma. In 1964 the Home Economics Building was rededicated as Chandler Hall to honor Sarah Chandler Hartsock.

The Kansas State Normal School.

Auxiliary Manual Training School.

———

First Annual Commencement.

Pittsburg, Kansas,

School Hall,

10 a. m., Monday, June 6, 1904.

Program.

———

Prayer, Rev. Geo. W. Trout.

Music.

The Province of Domestic Science, . . Pressie Chandler.

Rise and Progress of Manual Training, . Myrtle Graham.

Demonstration in Cookery—Salads, . { Mabel Robson. Anne Ranney.

Order of Work, ... Ethel M. Ollis.

Music.

Educational Advantages of Manual Training, Clara Belle Fair.

Demonstration in Cookery—Sandwiches, { Carrie Lyon. Margaret Herdman.

How Tools Assist in Education, . . Goldine Denton.

The Influence of Domestic Art in Schools, Gussie E. Sears.

Class Song.

Class Address, . . . President Jasper N. Wilkinson.

Presentation of Diplomas, . . . Supt. A. H. Bushey, Vice-president Board of Regents.

Benediction, Rev. Hugh McBirney.

ABOVE: Members of the Students Boarding Club rented this two-story house at 604 North Walnut Street, where their room and board averaged less than $2.25 per week. Students of the normal school often lived in cooperative boarding houses or rented rooms in private residences because the campus provided no housing until 1924.

OPPOSITE: Ten young women composed the first graduating class of the State Manual Training Normal School Auxiliary of Pittsburg. Each graduate received a manual training teaching certificate in June 1904. Left to right: Anne Ranney, Goldine Denton, Sarah Chandler, Ethel Ollis, Mabel Robson, Margaret Herdman, Myrtle Graham, Augusta (Gussie) Sears, Carrie Lyon, and Clara Belle Fair. Each taught school in Kansas after graduation. Sarah Chandler taught at the Manual Training Normal, and Myrtle Graham, Margaret Herdman, Mabel Robson, and Ethel Ollis were employed in the Pittsburg city schools. Goldine Denton went to Junction City, Clara Fair taught in Cherokee County, Carrie Lyon taught in Lawrence, Anne Ranney went to Miami County, and Augusta Sears taught in Parsons.

Program of the first commencement exercise, held on June 6, 1904. Each of the ten female graduates contributed a demonstration or presentation during the program. Jasper N. Wilkinson, president of the State Normal School in Emporia and the Manual Training Normal School Auxiliary, addressed the class.

Basketball was the first sport taken up by the students at the Manual Training Normal. On October 3, 1903, the *Pittsburg Daily Headlight* recorded that "a good basketball room has been arranged on the third floor [of Central School] and . . . the teams have been playing every evening." The first game to be played against an outside team was the normal against Pittsburg High School in January 1904. The high school team won the first meeting 10–6. A women's team was organized at the normal in November 1904. Professor Edwin Shepardson (standing second from right) coached the women's team in 1905.

An early paper bookmark
distributed as an advertisement.

OPPOSITE: The curriculum at the Manual Training Normal expanded quickly in 1904. Students met for mandatory chapel services on Monday mornings but attended physical exercise classes the remainder of the week. Four sections of calisthenics and gymnastics provided for exercise with Indian clubs (top), dumbbells, wands (middle), freehand gymnastics (bottom), and marching.

A manual arts basketry class in 1904. Professor Albert Bumann stands at the rear of the class. The various departments in the manual training program were arranged to meet the requirements of all grades, from kindergarten through high school. Paper folding, weaving, clay modeling, wood carving, bead work, and many similar activities were part of the curriculum.

A student modeling in clay. Details of the human figure and the head were taught in the first-year modeling classes.

Chapter Two

STATE MANUAL TRAINING
NORMAL SCHOOL, 1903–1923

Education for social efficiency is the most important task
the state has ever undertaken.

George Edmund Myers

WHILE MOST regional normal schools experienced modest to moderate enrollment, the growth in that of the State Manual Training Normal School Auxiliary was nothing short of phenomenal. Seventy students were in attendance after only two months of operation. By comparison, the State Normal School at Emporia did not attract seventy students until its third year of operations, and the school established at Fort Hays in 1902 would have only thirty-five students enrolled by 1905. These enrollment numbers proved the viability of the Pittsburg experiment in manual and domestic training programs. When a ten-week session started in April 1904, ninety-seven students enrolled. The Central School building, never designed to accommodate such numbers in household and industrial programs, was bursting at the seams. To continue this initial success, supporters of the school knew it was time for action.

Ebenezer Porter introduced a bill in the State Senate in January 1905 asking for an increase in the appropriation for faculty and for funds to erect a new building for the Manual Training Normal. At the same time, opponents in and out of the legislature hoped to cripple the school by cutting its appropriation. Even Jasper Wilkinson, president of the Emporia Normal School, acted as though the Pittsburg Auxiliary was an unwanted baby left on his doorstep. Porter and his allies settled for a substitute appropriation that provided up to $10,000 to purchase a permanent campus.

A spirited competition among Pittsburg real estate agents ensued when the Kansas legislature passed the substitute appropriation bill in March 1905. An offer for thirty acres of present-day Lincoln Park was rejected. A second proposal for fifteen acres where Lakeside Elementary School now stands was also rejected. The most attractive offer to the Board of Regents came from the Broadway Park Improvement Company: $6,000 for 17 acres on the southern outskirts of Pittsburg. The tract extended east from Broadway and was bounded on the north by Cleveland Street and on the south by Lindburg Street. This land became the center of the present-day Pittsburg State University campus.

With the purchase of a campus, efforts to obtain a building again became the focus of school supporters. The crucial test came in 1907 as the enrollment surged

The students at the Manual Training Normal School participated in basketball in the fall of 1903. In the summer of 1904, a tennis court was built in the rear of the Central School building.

An athletic association was organized in the fall of 1907 with seventy charter members. In the summer of 1909, five acres were donated to the association for an athletic field. That fall, students erected a wooden grandstand. This photograph of the first athletic grandstand was printed in the 1910 student yearbook, and it shows students competing in intramural track and field events. The school's first intercollegiate track and field competition was held on the site in May 1911 against a college from Marionville, Missouri.

The Kansas state legislature appropriated $150,000 in March 1907 to construct the first building of the new State Manual Training Normal campus. Construction began almost immediately and the new building, known as The Main, was completed in late 1908. The faculty and students helped to complete the move from Central School during Christmas break. The building became known as Russ Hall in 1911 after Russell S. Russ was fired for trying to separate the school from the Normal School in Emporia.

despite inadequate space. Enrollment that year had exceeded 350 students, but the friends of the school knew it could not grow any larger at the present location. They also knew that if an appropriation for a new building was secured, the school's permanence was likely ensured. Enemies of the school recognized this as well, and they fought the measure in Topeka. Porter marshaled his forces in the Capitol, and on February 11, 1907, the Senate passed a $150,000 building appropriation for the school. After considerable debate, the House passed the measure on March 2, and Governor Edward Hoch signed it three days later.

When the news reached Pittsburg, the celebration was spirited. Hundreds of jubilant students and townspeople greeted Principal R. S. Russ at the Santa Fe depot when he returned from his successful lobbying in Topeka. In an impromptu celebration the following morning, a number of boisterous students met Russ as he left the post office. Russ was gathered up on the shoulders of the jubilant crowd and carried to the Central School building, where he was "deposited with great care" on the steps.

The construction of the first building on the new campus began in August 1907 and was completed in December 1908. During the Christmas recess of that

This early State Manual Training Normal pennant displayed the school colors. The first evidence of a school color is found in a March 1907 newspaper article that mentions that red decorations were used at a reception for Pittsburg legislators after their successful bid to get the Russ Hall appropriation. Between 1907 and 1910 the colors of crimson and white are noted as official school colors. It was on Commemoration Day in 1910 that crimson and gold first were identified as the school colors.

Vocal and instrumental groups performed regularly in the original Russ Hall auditorium. C. Guy Hoover was the conductor and director of the Music Department when this photograph was taken in 1910. The statue of Nike—the Winged Victory, a senior class gift to the school in 1906—is shown on the left side of the stage. Well over 100 students were involved in the music program by 1910 through coursework, the Glee Club, or the orchestra, or as private students taking instruction in piano or voice.

year the school left the crowded Central School building and moved into the new spacious, four-story structure that would soon become known as Russ Hall.

Almost from the founding of the Manual Training Normal there was tension between the leadership of the schools in Emporia and Pittsburg. Once the permanent, state-supported campus and building became a reality in Pittsburg, Russ openly campaigned to separate his school from the administrative authority of the State Normal School in Emporia. In 1911 a separation bill was introduced in the state legislature that would give the Pittsburg institution autonomy. The bill would ultimately prove demoralizing to the Pitts-

burg institution. Not only did the bill fail to pass the house, but the events surrounding the separation also cost Russ his job. The Kansas Board of Regents dismissed him from his position as principal of the Manual Training Normal in retribution for his involvement in the separation movement.

One of the last achievements of the Russ administration was to secure an appropriation for erecting a second campus building. Construction of the industrial and applied arts building (now known as White-sitt Hall) began in 1911 and was completed in the spring of 1913. Although Russ, the founder of the State Manual Training Normal, had been removed, the school he built carried his legacy forward, through

The baseball team of 1910 was coached by John W. Fuhrer, the first director of the Department of Physical Education. Fuhrer came to the Manual Training Normal in 1907 from Wisconsin and remained at the school until his resignation in 1919.

change and challenge, into the twenty-first century. On May 31, 1911, Russ addressed faculty and students in the assembly hall. "This school has been too dear for me and the work too pleasant," he said, "for me ever to feel at home in another school. So I shall leave the profession of teaching for awhile anyway and perhaps for good." As Russ concluded, the audience began to sing the school song and the entire student body filed past, each student tossing a single red rose at the principal. Half a bushel of rose petals was dropped from a sheet suspended over where Russ stood.

In September 1911, the Kansas Board of Regents appointed George Edmund Myers as principal. Speaking about the school in his inauguration address, Myers noted that "in the eight brief years of existence its remarkable growth to an institution of nearly eleven hundred students and a faculty of thirty

members has challenged the attention of educators all over the state and far beyond its borders. Its rapid growth is evidence at once of the wisdom of those who were responsible for its establishment and of its need in the educational organization of the state." Clearly Myers himself believed in the value and quality of his predecessor's work. Though it would come at a high price for him as well, Myers would eventually achieve the objective that had cost Russ his position.

Myers was appointed to carry out the policies of the Board of Regents explicitly and, board members hoped, to quell the turmoil caused by Russ's dismissal. In retrospect, Myers's greatest accomplishment at Pittsburg was reorganizing the curriculum into a four-year course. The reorganization meant that every graduate would hold a degree, the same as any other college's graduates. The stigma of the teaching

The first inauguration at the State Manual Training Normal occurred on November 17, 1911, to install George Edmund Myers as the second principal. Myers, an Iowa native, received degrees from Ottawa University in Kansas, the University of Chicago, and Clark University in Worcester, Massachusetts. He taught at the Bacone Indian School in Muskogee, Oklahoma, and served as a high school principal in Colorado Springs, Colorado, and Washington, D.C., before coming to Pittsburg. Myers's tenure at Pittsburg remains the shortest of any principal or president, ending after two years as a consequence of the school's separation from the Normal School in Emporia.

Byron Reed, a right halfback and quarterback, participated on the football team in 1910 and served as vice president of the Manus Verez Literary Society. The students played intramural football as early as 1904 but the first Normal School football team was organized in October 1908. The first game was played against a Pittsburg High School team on October 2, 1908.

The student production of *The Mikado,* under the direction of C. Guy Hoover, was given at the LaBelle Theater in Pittsburg on February 28, 1911, following "some six weeks of faithful, strenuous work." This famous Gilbert and Sullivan comedy was the first operatic production undertaken by the school's Music Department.

These members of the male Glee Club in 1911 performed in *The Mikado* and other recitals throughout the year.

Before they were destroyed during the tragic fire of 1914, these wooden stairs in Russ Hall greeted students and guests. In this photograph several of the earliest senior class gifts, all statues lost in the fire, are seen at the top of the stairs.

certificate issued at the end of a two-year program was removed. Many of the Pittsburg graduates holding the certificates re-enrolled in 1912 to become members of the first baccalaureate class of 1913.

During the Myers administration, partisans of the Pittsburg school renewed the demands for separation from the Emporia normal. George Hodges, an outspoken friend of the Manual Training Normal, was elected governor in 1912. With Hodges's blessing, the 1913 state legislature abolished the normal school's Board of Regents. A newly appointed Board of Administration proceeded to separate the state normal schools and provided a clean slate by dismissing both Joseph Hill, president of the State Normal School of

Emporia, and Myers, principal of the Manual Training Normal.

The rancor created by the separation movement between Pittsburg and Emporia inspired lively commentary in the local newspapers. An editorial in the student newspaper the *Manualite* in February 1913 expressed the feelings of many in Pittsburg toward the Emporia Normal School:

> The tariff on lemons has been reduced since the One Board Bill and Separation is a realization and no longer a dream. We have our back yard so full of sour lemons that have been handed to us by our Stepmother, that rather than return them and pay the tariff we found it more profitable to let them rot

The beautiful marble stairway leading from the main entrance of Russ Hall to the second floor was added during the reconstruction of the building in 1915. Faculty, alumni, and students led a campaign to save the marble stairs in 1999 when Russ Hall renovation plans called for their removal. The university received an award from the Kansas Preservation Alliance in 2002 to honor its work in preserving this historic staircase.

where they fell and use them as fertilizers on our own soil. However the last one was so neatly packed in tinfoil that it arrived without a bruise and had the appearance of a Sweet Morsel—a graduation sheep skin—a full divorce with alimony—but it contained a flavor entirely unsuited to the digestion of SMTN. We might thrive for a time strapped down like a papoose, but when the straps are getting too tight we want to be free and discover when we pull aside our skirts that our feet are bound worse than those of a Chinese lady. So sure was our Stepmother that the last lemon would be devoured, rind and all, that she published a beautiful description of it in her Record

"binding us closer," "legislating our scope." The present legislature gave the guardians of SMTN the pleasure of returning this lemon to the sender C.O.D.

In July 1913 the Board of Administration created the office and title of president for the head of the now-independent State Manual Training Normal School. "Auxiliary" was no longer a part of the school's name. After a careful search, the board members elected William A. Brandenburg, then superintendent of the public schools in Oklahoma City,

Sixty members of the student opera troupe traveled to Chanute, Kansas, where they staged a performance of *The Chimes of Normandy* in November 1912. The troupe made appearances in six southeast Kansas communities that fall.

Students walked on dirt paths in 1913 as they passed by the new heating plant.

William Aaron Brandenburg was the first leader of the institution to hold the title of president. Appointed in 1913, he served until his death in 1940, making him the longest tenured president in the school's history. Brandenburg, an Iowa native, began his professional career as a teacher in a one-room log schoolhouse. He later earned degrees from Drake University in Des Moines, Iowa, and served as superintendent of schools in Mason City, Iowa, and Oklahoma City, Oklahoma, before coming to Pittsburg. Brandenburg was particularly admired by the students, who affectionately referred to him as "Prexy" throughout his entire tenure.

to be the first president of the Kansas State Manual Training Normal School.

Before Brandenburg completed his first year in office, on June 30, 1914, lightning struck Russ Hall. With most of the building and contents a complete loss from the resulting fire, Brandenburg led a community-wide drive to reconstruct the building and ensure the school's continuation. Financial pledges from Pittsburg residents and businesses in excess of $100,000 were received in the first thirty-six hours after the fire. Russ Hall was quickly rebuilt and re-dedicated in October 1915.

Brandenburg oversaw the construction of fourteen additional buildings during his twenty-seven-year presidency, which lasted until 1940. Before the State

Manual Training Normal period ended in 1923, the science hall named for Governor Thomas Carney was completed in 1919; the Physical Plant was finished in 1920; the Frances Willard dormitory for women, the cafeteria, and the gymnasium were completed in 1922; and Brandenburg Field and Stadium was nearing completion. Another major achievement of the Brandenburg administration was to further raise the academic standards of the institution and transform the Manual Training Normal School into a more complete liberal arts college. The public recognition of this accomplishment came in 1923 when the state legislature authorized a name change to Kansas State Teachers College of Pittsburg.

The advanced students in the Domestic Arts Department studied the latest fashions and were required to produce everything from simple underwear to the most complex and elaborate dresses. A course in millinery consisted of designing and making buckram and wire frames, plus covering and trimming winter and spring hats.

INDUSTRIAL ARTS BUILDING

A sketch of the Industrial Arts Building by student John Gilbert Wilkins appeared in the yearbook, the *Kanza,* of 1913. Wilkins was appointed an assistant professor of freehand drawing at Pittsburg from 1914 to 1920. He received his baccalaureate degree from Pittsburg in 1920 and then became an instructor at the Chicago Art Institute for many years. Wilkins's accomplishments included publishing a book, *Research Design in Nature,* and producing numerous drawings used in magazine advertisements for General Motors and other corporations.

In the early part of the twentieth century, May Day festivals were still common in many American communities. Members of the sophomore class of 1913 organized the first official May Day celebration on campus. In 1914 students danced around the maypole on the west lawn of Russ Hall to honor the May Queen, Helen Columbia, of Coffeyville, Kansas.

Summer school students and the faculty pose before the remains of Russ Hall following the fire of June 30, 1914. At 8:00 A.M. on the day of the fire, President William Brandenburg made a pledge to the anxious students that "SMTN would carry on." By 10:00 A.M., students, faculty, and townspeople had gathered at the Orpheum Theater and plans had been made for temporary classroom and office space.

After a fire destroyed most of Russ Hall in 1914, students used tents and downtown buildings as classrooms. When the Pittsburg streetcar workers went on strike, students were transported downtown in horse-drawn wagons.

An electric wiring class at work in the Industrial Arts Building in 1915.

Several of the student boarding houses in Pittsburg were featured in the 1915 *Kanza* yearbook.

The first student newspaper appeared in 1910 as the *Manual Normal Light*. In 1913 the title was changed to the *Manualite*. Georgia Lee Howard was editor-in-chief of the *Manualite* in 1915. Left to right: James Eldridge, literary editor; Nina Faye Waldrop, joke editor; S. Joe Williams, business manager; Georgia Lee Howard, editor; Geraldine Otwell, assistant business manager; Arthur Shumaker, athletic editor; Blanche Payne, society editor; and Hattie Farmer, alumni editor.

The Agriculture Club was organized on campus in 1912 and the Department of Agriculture was created in 1915. The club met every Wednesday at noon for a luncheon and program on some aspect of agriculture or rural life. Members of the club posed for this photograph in 1915.

ABOVE: In the spring of 1911, a student committee made plans for the first annual all-day school picnic. The destination was Noel, Missouri, approximately 100 miles south of Pittsburg on the Elk River. That first year a special Kansas City Southern train took 216 members of the senior and junior classes plus ten faculty sponsors to the picnic. Sara Stephens attended the annual picnic in May 1916 and photographed this group of young men she dubbed "the Jolly Six." By the 1920s these school picnics were held at Lake Taneycomo. From 500 to 1,500 students, alumni, and friends attended each year during the 1920s.

Football

A 1917 student yearbook illustration. Athletic lettermen in this early period were members of the "M" club and proudly displayed the letter *M* on their sweaters to represent the Manual Training Normal.

ABOVE: The Music Department presented Handel's Messiah annually from 1915 to 1947 as part of the spring music festival. This 1917 performance, under the direction of Walter McCray, was staged in the temporary auditorium that was constructed after the Russ Hall fire.

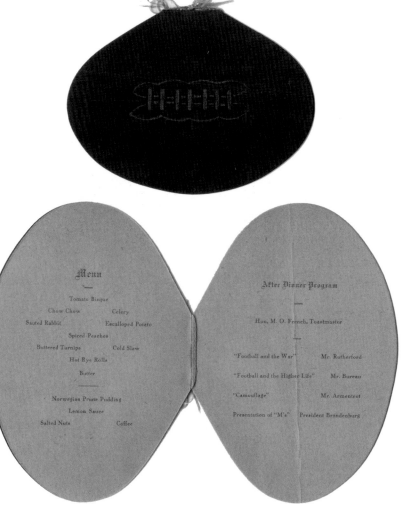

A souvenir program from the sixth annual football lettermen's dinner, held in December 1917.

Students, faculty members, and residents of southeast Kansas enlisted in large numbers during World War I. Batteries C and D of the 130th Field Artillery were mustered into service and barracked on the campus. For several weeks in early 1917, the campus was known as Camp Brandenburg. The Industrial Arts Building, now Whitesitt Hall, served as a guardhouse. To the left, the wood auditorium and cafeteria structures served as a mess hall and barracks. The rooms of the Commercial and Business Department in Russ Hall served as the officers' quarters. In this photograph, Battery D poses on the original athletic field where Carney Hall would be located two years later.

Members of the faculty assembled at this shelter on Cleveland Street on Friday afternoons to wait for the electric interurban trolley cars to take them to their various weekend extension classes in communities throughout the region.

Members of the Student Army Training Corps Band pose in front of Russ Hall in 1918. The Training Corps, founded during World War I, was a precursor for the later Reserve Officers' Training Corps programs on college and university campuses.

A machine shop class in the Industrial Arts Building in 1919.

The just-completed Carney Hall auditorium stage as it appeared in 1919. When Carney Hall was completed, it housed the departments of Home Economics, Chemical and Physical Sciences, Biology, and Agriculture. The auditorium, with a seating capacity of nearly 3,000, hosted numerous lectures, concerts, and plays until the building's deteriorating foundation caused it to be vacated in 1978.

1921
HEADQUARTERS
SODA
CANDY
S. M. T. N. School Supplies
TEXT BOOKS
(All Books at List Price)
COLLEGE INN
TOILET ARTICLES
STATIONERY

An ink blotter and calendar for 1921.

Coach Garfield W. Weede (standing third from left) and the 1921 track and field team. George Sweatt (standing center) from Humboldt, Kansas, was the Normal School's first black letterman. Sweatt earned letters in football, basketball, and track and field before receiving his teaching certificate from Pittsburg in 1922. After graduation Sweatt played professional baseball in the Negro National Leagues and holds the distinction of having played in the first four Negro Leagues World Series. From 1922 through 1925, Sweatt played infield and outfield for the Kansas City Monarchs. In the 1926 and 1927 seasons, Sweatt played for the Chicago American Giants.

The Arden Players, a student theatrical group under the direction of J. R. Pelsma, in 1921 presented a three-act comedy written by James Montgomery. The aim of the club, when it was founded in 1919, was "to produce the best amateur plays obtainable." *Nothing But the Truth* tells the story of a young stockbroker who believes honesty is the best policy in every instance. Members of his brokerage firm wager $10,000 that the young broker cannot speak the truth, exclusively, for a twenty-four-hour period. This popular production ran for 332 performances on Broadway in New York, was made into the musical *Yes, Yes, Yvette* in 1927, and later became a 1941 movie starring Bob Hope and Paulette Goddard.

The construction of Brandenburg Field and Stadium began in 1922 and was completed two years later. When it seemed a state appropriation for a permanent stadium was impossible to obtain, the Stadium Committee solicited donations from students, alumni, faculty, and Pittsburg citizens. It is said that the stadium was built by virtual slave labor, as each male faculty member was required to contribute several hours each week to work on its construction. The erection of Carney Hall, the gymnasium, and the cafeteria made necessary the relocation of the original athletic field and the wooden bleachers.

A manual arts sewing class in the 1920s.

A manual arts cooking class in the 1920s.

In 1920 student organizations held their first annual Stunt Fest. The faculty and students staged musical and vaudevillian entertainments to raise money for athletics and student publications. The event's popularity increased the next year with the addition of "Hobo Day." Men and women alike used the festive opportunity to dress like "knights of the road." Many of them posed in 1921 for this photograph, taken in Carney Hall auditorium.

Chapter Three

TRADITIONS AND SPIRIT

Let us greet the gold and crimson, with a strong and cordial cheer;
let our hearts be ever loyal to our Alma Mater dear.

Pittsburg State University Alma Mater,
words by Lena Martin Smith

THE STUDENT EDITORS of the 1960 *Kanza* yearbook wrote, "An organization without traditions is not a complete organization." Now, almost fifty years later, there are several recognizable traditions well associated with Pittsburg State University. One of the oldest and most distinctive traditions on the campus is Apple Day, a celebration that has occurred every year since 1907.

In 1905 Russell S. Russ, school founder, and the school's supporters in the Kansas legislature secured an appropriation to purchase land for a campus. In 1907 Russ returned to the legislature lobbying for funds to construct the first building on the new campus. While the legislature was in session, Russ sat in the chair of one of the legislators. Faculty members from the State Manual Training Normal and Clarence Price, the mayor of Pittsburg, were also on the floor. For these improprieties, the Pittsburg delegation was fined a barrel of apples, which was purchased and distributed among the members of the legislature. Historical accounts are unclear whether Russ or Price actually received the fine.

History is clear, however, that when the triumphant Russ returned to Pittsburg with news of the appropriation he called a school assembly at which the student body fined the faculty a barrel of apples. Despite a certain lack of logic, the story was circulated in virtually every newspaper in the state. The coverage attracted wide attention to the fact that there was a school devoted to training domestic and industrial arts teachers in Pittsburg and that it was going to have a fine new building.

The commemoration of the building appropriation was celebrated the following year in 1908 and a tradition was born. Commemoration Day, always known as Apple Day, became a major event on campus and throughout Kansas. A keynote address by the governor, or someone prominent in business or education, made each Apple Day convocation a featured event in the Kansas press for many years. Only with the onset of the Depression of the 1930s did notables generally cease to attend. For many years after 1930, the Apple Day program featured student organizations and pageants celebrating the college's history. In the 1950s the Apple Day convocation was followed by an all-school dance in the gymnasium and the selection of an Apple Day king and queen. In 1953 the Outstanding Senior Man and Woman awards were inaugurated as part of the Apple Day celebration. In the late 1970s the annual recognition of outstanding teachers was added to the

Students receive apples at the annual Commemoration Day program in Carney Hall in 1935, where women from the senior class distributed the fruit.

Apple Day events and in recent years student leadership awards have been given.

The earliest tradition of all at Pittsburg State University began with the thirty-three graduates of the class of 1906. They instituted the tradition of a senior-class gift to the school, stemming from the close bonds that developed between the school's leaders and the institution's students. The first gift was a full-size replica of the Winged Victory statue, which represented the Greek goddess Nike. The gift was reproduced by the firm of Caproni & Brothers of Boston, Massachusetts, from the original statue found in the Louvre in Paris, France. The 1906 graduates felt that the difficult struggle to establish a school in Pittsburg could best be commemorated by the world's most famous symbol of victory.

The forty-one members of the class of 1907 followed suit with a replica statue of Apollo, patron of the arts. Nike and Apollo were joined in 1908 by a replica of Minerva, the goddess of wisdom. When

Russ Hall was dedicated, these three impressive statues stood at the head of the stairs on the second-floor landing. Unfortunately, these statues were all lost in the 1914 Russ Hall fire. In the years since, however, the senior-class gifts have included others high in aesthetic qualities. The marble decorations that were placed above the west entrance to Brandenburg Field in 1924, for example, are the work of the renowned sculptor Waylande Gregory. Other gifts have become campus landmarks, such as the 1965 statue of the university's gorilla mascot located in front of the Overman Student Center.

Like colleges and universities everywhere, Pittsburg State has a tradition of homecoming celebrations. In the beginning, schoolwide reunions occurred at the annual teachers' meetings held on campus. As many as 3,000 people would attend these meetings each fall where the greeting of old friends was somewhat of a hidden benefit. By the 1920s the campus sororities and fraternities were hosting informal reunions. By the

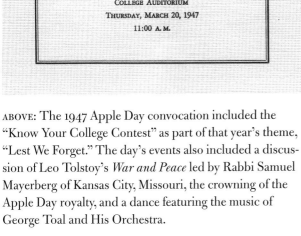

FORTY-FIRST ANNUAL

APPLE DAY

KANSAS STATE TEACHERS COLLEGE
PITTSBURG, KANSAS

COLLEGE AUDITORIUM
THURSDAY, MARCH 20, 1947
11:00 A. M.

ABOVE: The 1947 Apple Day convocation included the
"Know Your College Contest" as part of that year's theme,
"Lest We Forget." The day's events also included a discus-
sion of Leo Tolstoy's *War and Peace* led by Rabbi Samuel
Mayerberg of Kansas City, Missouri, the crowning of the
Apple Day royalty, and a dance featuring the music of
George Toal and His Orchestra.

ABOVE RIGHT: In 1952 the Apple Day Queen, Edith Land,
shares an apple with King Duane Lawellin. Land was
already the apple of Lawellin's eye, as the couple were
engaged to be married.

RIGHT: Charles Thomas celebrates Apple Day in a personal
way in 1958.

The tradition of senior class gifts began in 1906 with this replica statue of the Greek goddess Nike. This, like other early gifts, was destroyed in 1914 in the Russ Hall fire.

1930s, however, homecoming had become an important tradition on the fall calendar and had established a definite connection to a football contest. Sorority and fraternity house decorations lent to a festive atmosphere. A Friday-night bonfire and pep rally ended with students and alumni holding a snake dance through Pittsburg's business district. Halftime of the Saturday football game was filled with stunts and music, and large numbers attended a postgame banquet and dance in the college cafeteria.

Other campus gatherings throughout the years enhanced the camaraderie among the faculty and stu-

dents alike. The schoolwide picnics, watermelon feeds during summer school sessions, the long-ago Trout Bake held for male members of the faculty, and the present-day Faculty Association steak fry are but a few of the social events that have engendered a tradition of goodwill among the members of the Pittsburg State University family.

Cheerleaders, pep clubs, spirit squads, mascots, and pep bands have always played an important role in building camaraderie and support for the athletic teams of Pittsburg State University. Pep rallies before the games and events such as the "Yell Like Hell" contest on homecoming weekend have long been student and alumni favorites.

Rooting for the home team during the State Manual Training Normal period was a prominent feature of each athletic contest and was often covered in local news stories as extensively as the game. The coverage of a Thanksgiving Day football game in 1911 was no exception. A crowd of 700 fans watched the contest between Pittsburg and the Springfield (Missouri) Normal School. The campus newspaper *Manual Normal Light* (December 1911) reported that "fully a half hour before the game opened the Normal Boosters perched themselves, en masse, upon the rooters' bleachers on the east side of the athletic field. Songs and cheers followed each other rapidly. It is said that the rooting was the best and most spontaneous in the history of the school."

Until 1926 the elected yell leaders were all men, with one exception. According to newspaper accounts, in 1914 Miss Blanche Payne served as a cheerleader. One early yell leader was Harold "Babe" Alyea, who was also an all-conference center on Pittsburg's basketball team as a freshman, and a member of the track and field team. Alyea's greatest legacy at Pittsburg, however, was the founding of an all-male pep squad in October 1920 whose members called themselves the Gorillas. The Gorillas oversaw the sale of season tickets, made arrangements for special excursion trains to out-of-town games, sponsored rallies, picnics, and parades, and worked diligently on the fund-raising and construction of the football stadium that opened in 1924. On January 15, 1925, the student body voted to use the gorilla as a name and mascot for all the college's athletic teams. Pittsburg

Members of the faculty in 1919 enjoy themselves at one of the many college picnics held in Pittsburg's Lincoln Park. Left to right: C. S. Risdon, David Bowen, Oris P. Dellinger, J. F. Barnhill, Winfield Armentrout, Edgar Mendenhall, and James F. Mitchell.

President Rees Hughes carves up a watermelon for members of the faculty and the student body at the annual summer school watermelon feed.

In October 1920, twenty-four students under the leadership of Harold "Babe" Alyea organized themselves as the Gorillas to accelerate college spirit and enthusiasm until it permeated the state. Membership in the all-male pep squad quickly grew to over 100. Alyea was an athletic star for Pittsburg, lettering in basketball and track and field before transferring to the University of Chicago. Harold's brother, Paul, was a member of the football and the track and field teams and later served as an assistant coach at the college.

State remains the only college or university in the nation to have the gorilla as its mascot.

The female students were not to be outdone in showing support for the college. In 1920 the ladies formed their own pep squad to cooperate with the Gorillas. Known first as the Boosterettes, the women adopted the name Kampus Kats for their organization in 1923. The use of the Ks in their name was consistent with the change of the school's name in that year from State Manual Training Normal to Kansas State Teachers College. To mark the organization's new name, members composed an original song to the tune of "Sittin' in a Corner," with this chorus:

Just a bunch of coeds called Kampus Kats
Just a bunch of coeds with gaudy hats
We try to keep in step
And we're always full of pep
We help build up the rep of K.S.T.C.
Just a bunch of coeds to boost along
With loyal rooting and cheery song
We have some tall girls and some short girls
Some slender and some fats—just a bunch of coeds
Called Kampus Kats.

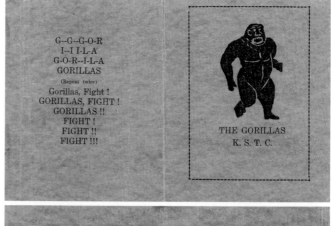

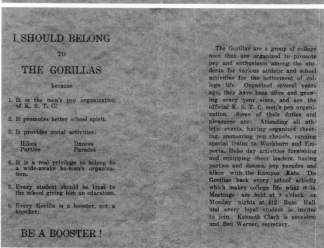

A women's pep club, known as the Kampus Kats by 1923, cooperated with the Gorillas in all pep rallies, cheers, and stunts.

BELOW AND OPPOSITE: Recruiting materials for the Gorillas in 1924 and for the Kampus Kats in 1927.

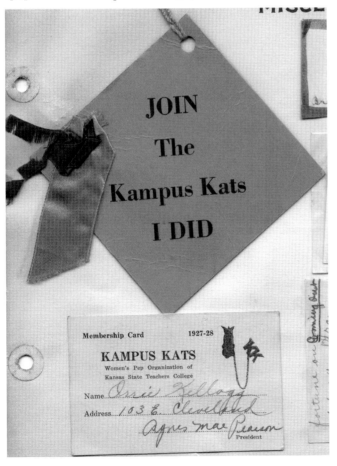

In 1938 the separate men's and women's pep clubs merged into one organization. At the men's basketball game against Wichita University in February, the members of the Pep Club made their first appearance in new crimson sweaters with gold gorilla emblems. The cheerleaders that year— Jack Overman, Jane Baxter, Jack Henderson, Betty Jo Coulter, and Albert "Frenchie" Delmez— wore gold sweaters with large crimson *K*s on the front.

World War II brought about many changes on the campus, including changes in the Pep Club's role. The 1942 and 1943 student yearbooks noted that pep and school spirit were "what the school needed and since everyone looked so down-in-the-mouth about the present emergency, the Pep Club set about to give the students just that." The Pep Club thought more activities were the answer, so its members "sponsored dances, bonfire rallies, a trip to a game in Springfield, Missouri, and many assembly programs. Pep during wartime is hard to promote," the editors noted, "but the pep club has done a fine job in building morale on the campus this year."

From 1920 to the early 1970s, commencement was held in the auditorium of Carney Hall or in the football stadium. It was traditional during those years for the faculty and graduating students to take a final walk around the campus Oval on their way to the commencement exercises. In recent times graduation ceremonies have been in the Garfield Weede Physical Education Building.

Master's degree candidates in industrial education in July 1936. Left to right: Harold Preston of Lawrence; Kenneth Pettit of Iola; Clarence White of Humboldt; Edwin Brychta of Osawatomie; Robert Sanders of Madison; Fred Rose of Liberal; and Ralph Collins of Kansas City, Kansas.

Two English majors, Orrie Kellogg (left) and Faye Williams (right), pause for this snapshot just before commencement exercises in 1936.

School spirit and student morale rebounded after World War II. In 1959, when Kansas State Teachers College became Kansas State College of Pittsburg, the Pep Club transitioned to an all-female organization known as the Pitt Peppers. Membership in the Peppers required attendance at all the athletic games and participation in halftime entertainments, and was a prerequisite for election to cheerleader. Traditions and organizations that featured uniformity were often challenged during the 1960s. The Pitt Peppers, with their matching crimson sweaters, were no exception and their reign on campus ended during the mid-1960s.

A souvenir from 1927.

The cheerleading squad continued to excel, however, and in the early 1970s Pitt State saw the reemergence of male cheerleaders.

By the late 1970s, a new era in school spirit had developed as a strong emphasis was placed upon the gymnastics and the physicality of cheerleading. Gus Gorilla and his partner, Gussie, were featured in many of the new routines and became crowd favorites. The Pride of the Plains Marching Band and the Pitt State Pep Band also contributed mightily to the activities. In 1980 the cheerleaders were further supported by pom-pom, flag, and twirler squads. From these groups the popular Crimson and Gold Dancers was formed in 1993.

Pittsburg State students have competed for national championships in cheerleading and dance every year since 1995. The Pittsburg State cheerleaders were second overall in 1998 and brought home a first-place finish in January 2001. The Crimson and Gold Dance team has also participated in the national competitions since 1999, finishing as high as third place in the 2000 event.

ABOVE: The 1,403 members of the senior class of 1971 joined more than 35,000 Pittsburg students who had graduated since 1904. Dr. Allan Ostar, executive director of the American Association of State Universities and Colleges, told them, "In the year 2000 you will all be doing jobs no one even knows about at this moment."

LEFT: An unidentified, but joyous, graduate in 1990.

ABOVE: In 1921 Dean George W. Trout instituted
an annual dinner for the male members of the
faculty. Dean Trout hosted the event, known
as the Trout Bake, until retiring in 1939. S. L.
Householder, Ron Smith, and John Lance, in
turn, hosted the tradition until it was discontin-
ued in the late 1970s. In this photograph, circa
1948, the cooks prepared the meal under the
east stadium bleachers. In the front row (left
to right) are Harry Hartman, Frank German,
L. L. Tracy, George Ruggles, and John Lance.
In the second row (left to right) are Robert
Hart, Ron Smith, unidentified, J. D. Haggard,
Charlie Dellasega, unidentified, Robert Noble,
S. L. Householder, and unidentified.

RIGHT: Coach Garfield "Doc" Weede shares
memories and a soft drink with his wife,
Ethyle Porter Weede, around 1966. The
couple, college sweethearts, married in
1907 following a seven-year engagement.

In 1933 William Brandenburg celebrated his twentieth anniversary as college president with guests in the campus cafeteria, later rededicated as Chandler Hall.

LEFT: Float construction in 1957. Left to right: Robert Trager, Dianna Cuppy, George Abbott, and Ken McManis were members of Sigma Tau Gamma fraternity and Sigma Sigma Sigma sorority.

OPPOSITE BELOW: Student Otto A. Hankammer, later a member of the industrial education faculty, sketched the scene as the Gorilla faithful gathered for the homecoming game against the College of Emporia in 1926.

The Alumni Association was organized on Commencement Day at the close of the school's first year. On June 6, 1904, the ten young women who became the first graduating class met in the sewing room of the Central School building and organized the association. Sarah Preswick Chandler was elected the first president. Alumni have returned to campus every year since for some type of reunion. In 1959 the alumni held their reunion banquet on the upper level of the Student Center.

LEFT: The cover of an early homecoming game program where Pittsburg was victorious over the opponent by a score of 7–0.

BELOW: Alpha Sigma Alpha house decorations for homecoming in 1960. The Washburn Ichabods were that year's football opponents.

OPPOSITE ABOVE: A 1946 homecoming parade float rolls by the 300 block of North Broadway in downtown Pittsburg.

OPPOSITE BELOW: Homecoming Queen Donna Guinn (center) in 1961 with her court (left to right) Darlene Crane, Charlene Crane, Carol Winkel, and Sherri Gill.

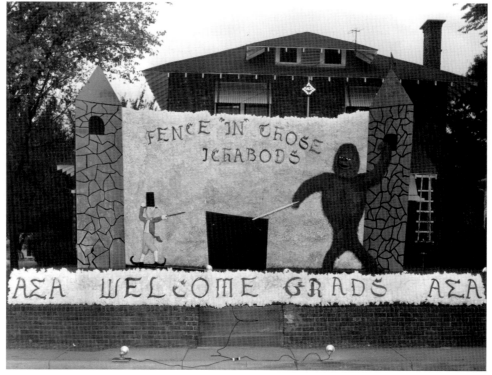

Pi Kappa Alpha's "Erector Set," with Queen candidate Genevieve Schaub, took first place in the 1967 Queen float division of the homecoming parade.

A 1969 homecoming souvenir.

This chalk statue of Massachusetts educator Horace Mann was the gift of the senior class of 1927. It was given in the same year that the Horace Mann building was opened as an elementary laboratory school. Horace Mann (1796–1859) is recognized as the father of normal schools in America. The statue stood in the main reference room of Porter Library until the library was moved to a new facility in 1979. The location of the statue is now unknown.

Relief sculptures of a football player and a discus thrower adorn Carnie Smith Stadium. The sculpture, a gift of the class of 1924, was executed by Waylande Gregory, a Pittsburg State University graduate and accomplished sculptor and ceramics artist.

The senior classes of 1993 through 1996 contributed to the construction of the Centennial Bell Tower, which was dedicated in October 2000. The new campus icon is located between the Axe Library and the football stadium on Joplin Street. The idea for the bell tower came from discussions about a project that would commemorate the university centennial and point the way to the university's second century.

ABOVE: The Gorillas pep club asked art student Helen Waskey to draw an image of a gorilla for them in 1922. This first depiction of what later became the school mascot was published in the 1923 *Kanza* yearbook.

RIGHT: On January 15, 1925, the student body unanimously adopted the gorilla as the mascot for all the Kansas State Teachers College athletic teams.

BELOW: No one recalls the exact moment when the mascot became known as Gus Gorilla, but the image of the gorilla changed frequently. In the early 1960s, for example, he became a regular "Joe College."

Today's popular and trademarked "split-face" gorilla image was created by graphic artist Michael Hailey in 1986. Ironically, Hailey has since worked for the Lions of archrival Missouri Southern State University in Joplin.

Yell leader S. Joe Williams, known to the student body as "Saint Joe," posed on the athletic field during the 1915 football season.

Lena Martin, a member of the first graduating class to receive the baccalaureate degree in June 1913, composed the original lyrics for the school song in 1910. "The Crimson and Gold" was first performed in public by the school choir at commencement exercises in 1911 and has been the official alma mater ever since. Because of changes to the university's name, the song's lyrics were revised in 1923, 1959, and 1979.

56

Female cheerleaders were officially elected for the first time on the campus in 1926. The squad that fall included (left to right) Jack Keller, Nadeane Cracraft, D. Marceitis Ware, Ruth Durbin, Charles Haddock, and Ralph Hoar. The only female cheerleader on record before 1926 was Blanche Payne in 1914.

President William Brandenburg participated in a November 1936 pep rally. Pittsburg went on to defeat Wichita State 7–0.

Cheerleader Katherine Bradshaw in 1963.

Jack Overman, cheerleader and senior class president in 1941, exhibited his boundless enthusiasm for his alma mater in 1967. Overman served as director of the student union from 1951 to 1984.

The cheerleaders in 1973 included (back row left to right) Jan Wade, Delores Brown, and Cindy Fauvergue; (front row left to right) Patty Knoll, Barbara Shiverdecker, Alana Rua, and Earlene Page.

Chapter Four

KANSAS STATE TEACHERS COLLEGE, 1923–1959

There is but one thing greater in this world than being a great teacher.
That one thing is being a truly worthy teacher of teachers.

William Aaron Brandenburg

WILLIAM AARON BRANDENBURG, who became the president of the State Manual Training Normal in 1913, set about to transform the institution from a school to a college. In the aftermath of the school's separation from the State Normal School in Emporia, his goals included expanding the curriculum, improving the faculty, increasing enrollment, expanding four-year degree programs, and constructing additional classroom buildings. Brandenburg's plans were temporarily modified in June 1914 when most of Russ Hall was destroyed by a tragic fire that claimed the life of one student, Rex Tanner.

Before the embers of Russ Hall had ceased smoldering, a mass meeting was held in Pittsburg's Orpheum Theater. There, state and school officials entered into an agreement to rebuild Russ Hall at once and to raise the necessary funds by popular subscription. Before thirty-six hours had passed, the business owners and citizens of Pittsburg had pledged $136,000 of their own money for the project. Governor George Hodges and the members of the Board of Administration agreed to recommend to the next state

legislature an appropriation to repay the money raised by pledges. The 1915 legislature appropriated $188,565.65 to refund the pledges and complete the building's restoration. This appropriation ended, finally, the long-standing challenges to the permanency of the school in Pittsburg.

Historian Robert Ratzlaff noted, "The first decade under President William Brandenburg may be described as a struggle for respectability as the normal school attempted to become a real institution of higher learning." Repeatedly, Brandenburg stressed to faculty, students, and the general public that for a teachers' college to fulfill its mission it had to have acceptable standards of scholarship, highly qualified faculty, and adequate facilities. By 1922 academic departments were more clearly organized, the enrollment had grown to 700 full-time students, and the faculty numbered ninety-three, most with advanced degrees. The sought-after respectability was officially recognized in 1923 when the institution became Kansas State Teachers College of Pittsburg. The administration and the faculty, according to Ratzlaff, "had worked diligently to build a teacher preparation

Brandenburg Field and the college's stadium were dedicated on Armistice Day, November 11, 1924. The college band helped the crowd cheer the team to an inaugural 12–2 victory over Friends University.

Students, faculty, alumni, and friends of the college initiated a drive for a new athletic field and stadium in 1922. To show their appreciation for the president's cooperation and enthusiasm, the backers of the project asked that the new facility be named after President William A. Brandenburg. Following major renovations in September 1989, the facility was rededicated as the Carnie Smith Stadium and William A. Brandenburg Field.

Ku Chui Huang and Jen Fak Woo from China (front row, third and fourth from the right) were the first international students to enroll at the college. They came to Pittsburg to study electrical engineering on the recommendation of a Mrs. Brewster, a missionary in China who was the cousin of Wilbur Mason, pastor of the First Methodist Episcopal Church in Pittsburg. In this photograph Huang and Woo appear with other engineering students and faculty members in 1924.

institution that offered a variety of courses of study. This was achieved primarily through a very comprehensive extension service, a very successful summer school program, and the increased respectability of teaching as a profession."

The struggle for maturity that led up to and continued throughout the teachers' college era prompted the first extensive expansion of the campus's physical facilities. In 1913, when Brandenburg became president, the campus contained only two buildings. When he died twenty-seven years later, there were thirteen major buildings on the campus. The struggle for maturity in those years also included adding a graduate school program in 1929 and creating important administrative positions, such as dean of men and dean of women. The college survived such significant challenges as low enrollments that occurred during the Depression of the 1930s and World War II. In 1934, in the depths of the Depression, 126 Pittsburg students were on the relief rolls but over 700 had applied for assistance. Most of the students on assistance worked fifty hours per month at the college, for which they earned $15.

The faculty and students, despite their economic circumstances, remained very active and intellectually engaged during the Depression. Professor Edgar Mendenhall spent one summer touring Russia. Marjory Jackson of the Music Department spent ten months abroad studying voice in Switzerland and Germany, and Elton Brown, a Pittsburg track star, spent a summer in Germany as a member of the Amateur Athletic Union track team. The college YMCA organized a series of talks on the European political situation, and Dr. Ernest Mahan of the History Department delivered the first talk, "Hot Spots in Europe." Debate flourished, as did football and basketball, and the Music Department, under the direction of Walter McCray, gave periodic concerts throughout the fall and spring. Gabby Street, a manager of the St. Louis Cardinals baseball team, gave a speech in the Music Hall auditorium. Conductor Karl Krueger brought the Kansas City Philharmonic Orchestra to perform in Carney Hall. Prohibition lecturers tried to make Pittsburg the driest campus in the nation, and Dr. Daniel A. Poling, editor of the *Christian Herald* magazine, and Homer Rodeheaver, pub-

Walter McCray (left) and William Aaron Brandenburg (right) met John Philip Sousa at the Missouri Pacific train station in October 1927. Large crowds greeted the "March King," who was visiting Pittsburg for the third time. Sousa, upon McCray's invitation, came to conduct five area high school bands in a matinee and evening performance in Carney Hall auditorium.

lisher of church music, gave a joint lecture-recital centering on the dry crusade movement.

The school year of 1934–1935 also saw many physical changes on the campus. The Russ Hall driveway was repaved, and what was described as the "ugly brick walls in front of Russ Hall" were removed so that the lawns could be terraced. Cleveland Avenue on the north side of the college was widened, and Chinese elms were planted on the lawn to replace the trees that had been removed. College Lake was finished and named, having been for years merely a pond that had served the farm that became the college campus in 1905. An observatory with a refracting telescope was constructed atop Russ Hall and a new loudspeaker system was installed in the press box at the stadium.

The commencement address for the 371 graduates of the class of 1935 was given by Dr. Walter B. Pitkin, head of the School of Journalism of Columbia University. Pitkin spoke about the need in difficult times for the rarest kind of teacher. "Every teacher," he said, "should so live that his pupils never suspect that he is teaching anything, while in reality he is teaching everything—the art of living, growing up, learning, keeping well, love, play, work, and the art of getting along with people." Pitkin's challenge to the students was reinforced by the comments of Brandenburg, who stated, "Better times are coming.... The diplomas you receive today signify that you are among an elite group. The faculty joins me in congratulating you upon your ambition, and your effort, and wishes you every good as you enter into a larger

The addition of the College Observatory on the roof of Russ Hall began in October 1926. The 10-inch refracting telescope was obtained by Professor J. A. G. Shirk from the Lohmann Manufacturing Company in Ohio. The observatory was dismantled in 1999 during the remodeling of Russ Hall.

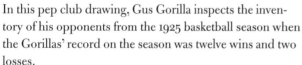

BOTANY—Drawing

The Day Lily 6-29/25

In this pep club drawing, Gus Gorilla inspects the inventory of his opponents from the 1925 basketball season when the Gorillas' record on the season was twelve wins and two losses.

A page from Zelpha Ruggles's notebook kept during the summer session of 1925.

field of service as brighter days return to our educational work."

Brandenburg opened his twenty-eighth year at the college in September 1940. He died in St. Mary's hospital in St. Louis on October 29 of that year after being in declining health for some months. Dr. Oris Polk Dellinger, dean of the College and Graduate School since 1929, served as acting president for the remainder of the academic year. Dellinger, one-time chairman of the Biology Department, was one of only four members of the faculty before 1923 to hold a PhD. On July 1, 1941, Dellinger relinquished his duties to the new president, Dr. Rees H. Hughes, who perhaps is best remembered for recruiting numerous highly qualified faculty members to the college over

the next sixteen years. But Hughes also oversaw the challenging years of World War II, when enrollment dropped, and the great enrollment increases occasioned by the passage of the GI Bill after the end of the war.

When World War II ended, the campus saw veterans return to the college in proverbial droves. Hughes announced that regular enrollment at the college in 1947 had reached an unprecedented 2,000 students with an additional 29 special music students, 224 children in the Horace Mann Laboratory School, 128 teenagers in College High School, and 681 correspondence students. In response to the growth, Hughes led the college through its second major period of construction, which began in the mid-1950s and lasted

Nine pairs of twins organized the Somos Gameles, better known as the Twins Club, on the Pittsburg campus October 29, 1925. This picture of the twins appeared in newspapers across the United States and in Canada and England. Seated left to right are Pansy and Violet Lewis; Caroline and Elizabeth Burke; Martha and Mary Gibson; Beatrice and Berenice Carter; and Velma Lee and Delma Dee Lough. Standing left to right are Max and Marie Lafferty; Charles and Theodore Wood; Earle and Merle Farnsworth; and Lillian and Lucile Tankersley. Somos Gameles reorganized in 1926 with eight pairs of twins; five sets continuing from the first year were joined by three new sets who enrolled at the college.

for a decade. Seven new dormitories, Hughes Hall, Yates Hall, and a classroom addition to Russ Hall were all opened by 1964. In that same fall of 1947, George Weiss, in an editorial in the *Collegio,* moaned that long skirts for women were coming back in fashion. "Frankly," he said, "they give all women the appearance of having piano legs, and actually of having forgotten to change from Grandmaw's nightie before coming to class. . . . Our last chance, men, is to appeal to the Supreme Court, but little it cares—it wears robes."

Hughes maintained the college's emphasis on teaching until his retirement in 1957. However, by that time many students were interested in more than teaching careers. In particular, enrollments in the Business and Industrial Arts departments were mov-

ing the institution away from teacher training and toward the liberal arts. Leonard H. Axe, appointed in 1957, brought a background in business administration to the presidency. Increased numbers of bachelor of arts and bachelor of science degrees were awarded along with the traditional baccalaureate degrees in education. In 1958 the college was authorized to offer a specialist in education degree, and in 1959 the master of arts degree was approved. Also in 1959, the *Midwest Quarterly,* an interdisciplinary journal of contemporary thought, replaced the teacher-oriented *Educational Leader* as the primary scholarly publication issued by the college. These changes in emphasis were formally recognized in that same year when "Teachers" was dropped from the institution's name and it became the Kansas State College of Pittsburg.

Sherwood, or *Robin Hood and the Three Kings,* by Alfred Noyes was dramatized in the stadium in July 1926 by the Department of Speech, with assistance from the Physical Education, Music, and Physical Science departments. A realistic Sherwood Forest was provided for Robin Hood and his merry men by placing an abundance of branches and shrubbery on the athletic field. Students from the Horace Mann elementary training school and live animals joined the troupe for the performance.

The Men's Glee Club of 1927 was under the direction of Walter McCray. Performances included the "Pilgrim's Chorus" from *Tannhäuser* and "Going Home" from Dvorak's New World Symphony.

Dorthy Kiddoo sweeps the back porch and Genevieve Hawkins hangs the laundry at the Home Management House in 1927. The house was completed in November 1926, and home economics majors enrolled in household administration lived there on a rotating basis. Groups of eight girls occupied the home for nine-week periods and were entirely responsible for the home's administration and upkeep.

The Home Management House on South Joplin Street as it appeared in 1930.

Red Cross Life-Saving Corps in 1928 at the gymnasium swimming pool. Front row from left to right: Thelma Cornelson, Mary Garlock, Veva J. Woodard, Eleanor Wilson, Eunice Wilson, Dorris E. Adams, Pricilla Waggoner, Helen Brandenburg. Back row from left to right: Dorothy Weede, Grace Ann Rocleu, Ruby Van Winkle, Hazel Cave, Thora E. Ludvickson.

A woodworking class in the Industrial Arts Building, circa 1930. Much of the classroom and library furniture for new buildings erected on the campus from 1919 to 1929 was built by students in these classes.

In the summer of 1931, 1,229 students were enrolled in the School of Education. A group prepares to leave on a field trip on one of two REO buses the college purchased in 1929.

Niles Smith (left) from Independence, Kansas, at the piano and Claude Lear from Harper, Kansas, holding the violin, probably 1929.

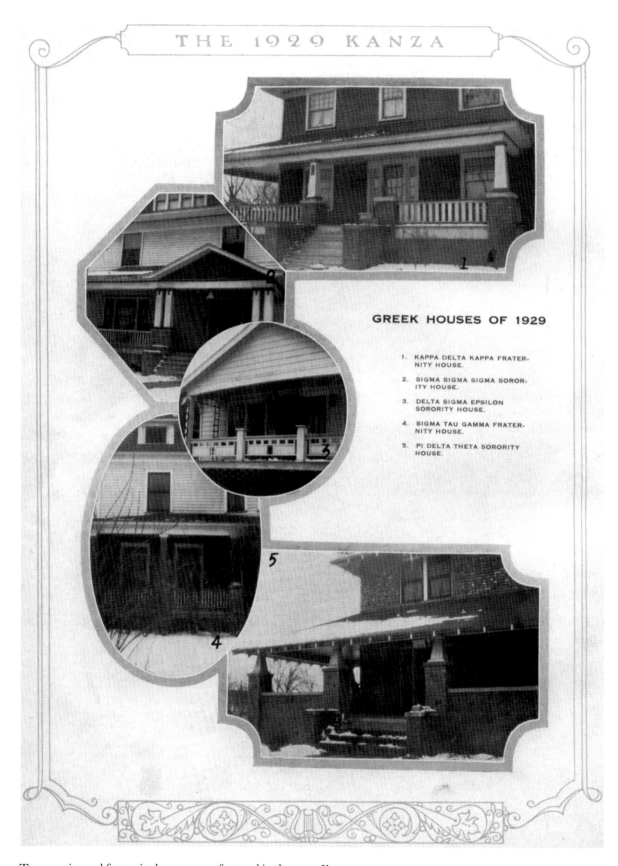

GREEK HOUSES OF 1929

1. KAPPA DELTA KAPPA FRATER-
   NITY HOUSE.

2. SIGMA SIGMA SIGMA SOROR-
   ITY HOUSE.

3. DELTA SIGMA EPSILON
   SORORITY HOUSE.

4. SIGMA TAU GAMMA FRATER-
   NITY HOUSE.

5. PI DELTA THETA SORORITY
   HOUSE.

Ten sorority and fraternity houses were featured in the 1929 *Kanza*.

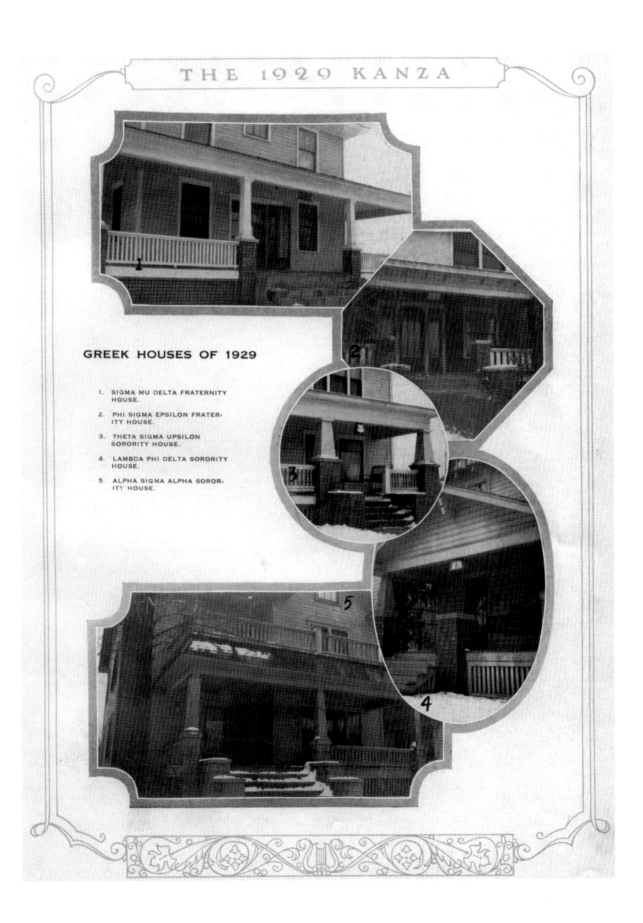

GREEK HOUSES OF 1929

1. SIGMA MU DELTA FRATERNITY
   HOUSE.

2. PHI SIGMA EPSILON FRATER-
   ITY HOUSE.

3. THETA SIGMA UPSILON
   SORORITY HOUSE.

4. LAMBDA PHI DELTA SORORITY
   HOUSE.

5. ALPHA SIGMA ALPHA SOROR-
   ITY HOUSE.

William Spendlove, landscape gardener for the campus from 1917 to 1944, stands in front of Whitesitt Hall in 1932. "Spinney," as he was known to students, moved to Pittsburg in 1905 and worked as a miner and a plumber before coming to the campus. Spendlove maintained the campus greenhouse and planted different specimens of trees native to Kansas on the campus during his tenure. He also propagated over fifty new varieties of flowers through cross-pollination of zinnias, including a crimson and gold variety he named the W. A. Brandenburg zinnia.

The financial and administrative secretaries in Russ Hall in October 1933. Belle Provorse (right foreground) was the secretary for presidents William Aaron Brandenburg and Rees Hughes from 1913 to 1954.

An Art Department model and drawing class in 1933. Artwork for the annual student Stunt Fest and Hobo Day celebration is seen in the background.

Elementary students of the Horace Mann Training School read about human geography and other subjects during library time in 1933. The laboratory school prepared college students to teach children in grades one through six until it was closed in 1971.

Walter McCray conducts the Kansas State Teachers College festival orchestra on the Carney Hall auditorium stage in 1933. McCray came to Pittsburg in 1914 as the second chairman of the Music Department. He started the college's annual Music Festival in 1915. A highlight of each festival until McCray retired in 1947 was the presentation of Handel's *Messiah*. A performance of the *Messiah* was part of the April 2008 celebration of the centennial of the founding of the Music Department.

"Why so glum, fellows? We'll get 'em in the second half." A locker-room scene during halftime of a game in 1933.

Alvin Proctor served as editor of the student newspaper, the *Collegio,* in 1934 and 1935. Proctor returned to the college in 1948 as a history professor and served as social science chairman from 1949 to 1959; graduate school dean from 1959 to 1968; executive vice president from 1966 to 1968; academic vice president from 1968 to 1978; and assistant to the president from 1978 to 1981. Members of the *Collegio* staff included (left to right) Irvin Luthi, Proctor, Jane Orr, and Clay DeFord.

Editor Carl Jackson (center) and members of the *Kanza* yearbook staff in 1935.

President William Brandenburg takes a spin with a faithful companion in 1935.

The college's boosters have never been accused of being fair-weather fans. The Pittsburg faithful watch a football game in 1935.

Shuffleboard courts were installed in the cafeteria annex in December 1936. These students were on hand to play the very first matches.

The Gorillas take the field in 1937. It was the final season for coach Edward "Blue" Howell, who ended his eight-year tenure with an overall record of thirty-five wins, thirty losses, and six ties. Howell was replaced by Charlie Morgan, who coached until the legendary Carnie Smith arrived in 1949.

The College Inn was a favorite student hangout for many years on East Cleveland Street. Joe Beitzinger, longtime manager, sold books, school supplies, and sundries in addition to food and drink.

Charles M. Miller (right), president of the college's Alumni Association, presented a new Graham automobile to William Aaron Brandenburg upon the twenty-fifth anniversary of Brandenburg's presidency, March 19, 1938. Brandenburg served as president from 1913 until his death in November 1940. His twenty-seven years in office continues to be the longest of any president in Pittsburg State University's history.

An Art Department painting class and model in 1942.

Two "dangerous" young women? Senior Nada Pauline
Van Landingham (left) and junior Dorothy Eyman
posed for this photograph in May 1938.

During World War II, some students learned to fly in a civilian pilot training course offered at the college. The faculty taught primary, secondary, cross-country, and apprentice instructor courses, and the student flyers had ten planes at their disposal ranging from Cubs to a five-passenger Stinson.

Students (left to right) Don Griffin, Alice Bennett, Fred Bumgarner, and Janet Hughes take a time-out from their studies in Porter Library in 1942.

The 1942 *Kanza* yearbook staff tried to make light of a serious situation in the early months of World War II.

What To Do
IN CASE OF AN AIR RAID

1. As soon as bombs start dropping, run like the dickens!
   (It doesn't matter where you run as long as you run like the dickens!)

2. Take advantage of all opportunities afforded you when air raid sirens sound.

   For example:
   (a) If in a bakery, grab a pie or cake.
   (b) If in a tavern, grab a bottle.
   (c) If in a movie, grab a blond.

3. If you find an unexploded bomb, always pick it up and shake it hard, the firing pin may be stuck. If this doesn't work, put it in the furnace, and let it warm up.

4. If an incendiary bomb is found burning in a building, throw some gasoline on it. You can't put it out anyhow, so you might as well have some fun.

5. Always get excited and holler like all getout. It adds to the confusion and scares the devil out of the kids.

6. Drink heavily, eat onions, limburger cheese, etc., before entering a crowded air-raid shelter. This will make you very unpopular with the crowd in your vicinity and eliminate any unnecessary discomfort that would be more prevalent if people crowd too closely.

7. If you should be the victim of a direct bomb hit, don't go to pieces! Lie still and nobody will notice you.

8. Smack the air-raid warden in the face if he starts to tell you what to do. They always save the best seats for themselves and their friends anyway!

BELOW: Lt. Clifton Harkins arrived at the college on June 1, 1943, to establish a U.S. Navy Officer Training Unit known as the V-12 program. The program's purpose was to give prospective naval officers the benefits of a college education in areas such as mathematics, English, history, physics, engineering, and naval organization. The Pittsburg State program had 645 participants before it was decommissioned on October 24, 1945, at the end of World War II.

Navy V-12 cadets stand in formation on the campus Oval in 1944.

The Otto Way, just one block from campus at 1402 South Broadway, was a popular hangout during World War II.

The ladies test their balance and flexibility in a physical education exercise in 1945.

Quonset huts were erected on campus during World War II to house the Navy V-12 cadets. The huts were converted to married-student housing in 1946, complete with small garden plots.

A chemistry student in a
Carney Hall laboratory
in 1947.

"Upholstery for Homemakers" was offered as part of the Smith-Hughes Vocational and Rehabil-
itation Program for World War II veterans in 1947. After World War II, the Smith-Hughes Vocational Education Act of 1917 addressed the need to transition veterans to a peacetime economy.

Arc-welding and metal shop were a popular part of the industrial education curriculum in 1947.

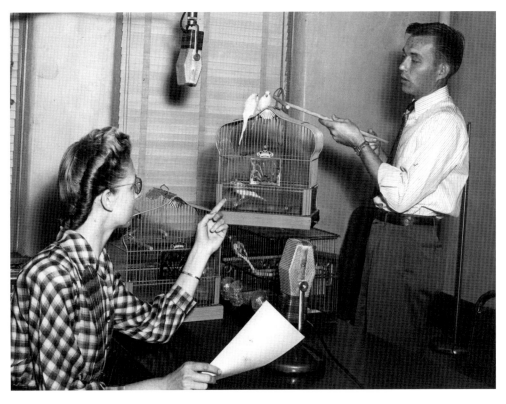

Broadcasting students in 1949 worked on campus and in the studios of KSEK radio in Pittsburg.

Members of the KSTC marching band in 1948.

LEFT: Garfield "Doc" Weede retired as athletic director and head of the Physical Education Department in 1947 but remained as track coach and instructor until 1957. Weede played football at the University of Pennsylvania and was a member of Walter Camp's All-American team of 1904. Weede practiced dentistry and coached at Washburn University and Sterling College in Kansas before coming to Pittsburg in 1919. At Pittsburg he also coached basketball until 1922 and football until 1929.

OPPOSITE: A weekly book talk program the college produced was broadcast over radio station KSEK. On April 7, 1949, the program featured a discussion of Thomas Merton's *Seven Story Mountain.* Program guests were Father Edward York, chaplain of the campus Newman Center; Margaret Haughawout, professor of English; Gilbert Fites Jr., circulation librarian for the college; and Angela deGagne, instructor of Spanish and French.

A shortage of student housing in 1948 forced the college to allow some married students to park their mobile trailers underneath the football stadium and beside the college lake.

James R. Wells, chairman of the Biology Department, instructed this nursing class. The college was associated with the Mt. Carmel School of Nursing until the Kansas Board of Regents authorized a four-year nursing program on campus in the spring of 1970.

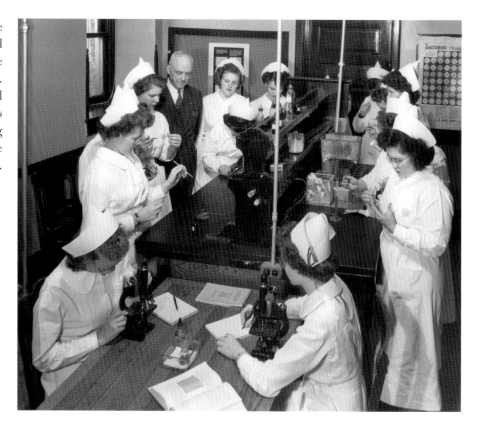

Enrollment was always a hectic time for students and faculty. President Rees Hughes (lower left) helps a student complete the process in 1950.

Robert W. Hart, professor of mathematics, enjoyed being the disc jockey for a musical recollections program that aired in the summer of 1950.

BELOW: President Rees H. Hughes and Isabel Hughes at home in 1952. Hughes was appointed the second president of the college in 1941. He steered the college through low enrollments in World War II by attracting naval training units to the campus, then oversaw the rapid growth in enrollments created by the GI Bill after the war. The student union, four dormitories, and a classroom addition to Russ Hall were built during Hughes's administration. He stepped down as president in 1957 but remained as a professor of education and psychology until 1961. After his retirement from the college, Hughes was elected to the Kansas state legislature.

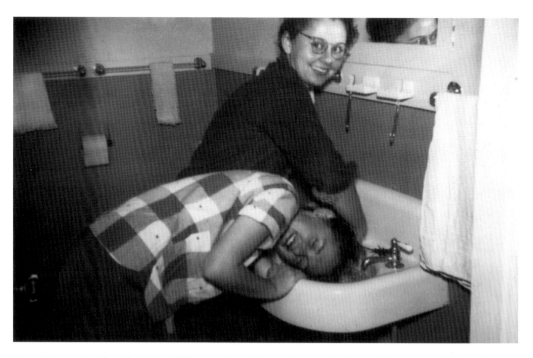

Betty Pacconi washes the hair of fellow student Aleeta Cass at the Home Management House in 1953.

This aerial view of the campus was taken during the fiftieth anniversary celebration in 1953.

The Home Economics Department kitchen as it looked in 1953. Home economics classes were held in Carney Hall for many years but in 1951, the old cafeteria building was remodeled for use by the department. The remodeled building was rededicated as Chandler Hall in 1964 to honor the department's first director, Sarah Chandler Hartsock.

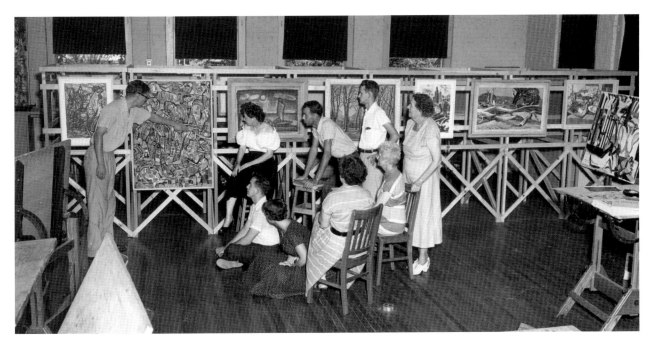

Eugene Larkin (left), art instructor, explains the abstract technique to students in 1953, including Gene DeGruson and Gayle Page, seated on the floor.

The *Gaudeamus Igitur* production from 1954 included this appealing line-up. *Gaudeamus Igitur* ("Let us rejoice, there-fore") is the common title of the longer work *De Brevitate Vitae*. It is regarded as the oldest recorded student song, based upon a Latin manuscript of 1287, and is often associated with graduation ceremonies. The college production occurred annually for about a decade under the direction of history professor Dudley Cornish.

The college's research farm, located approximately four miles west of Pittsburg, included a grape vineyard in 1955.

In 1954 Ellouise McVay became the first female sports editor for the student newspaper, the *Collegio,* in the school's history.

Gus Gorilla walks while the cheerleaders ride during the homecoming parade in 1954.

Returning lettermen run through the offense before the 1954 season. Left to right: Dave Fowler from Arcadia, Kansas; Bill Hollenbeck from Clay Center, Kansas; Ray McDaniel from Pittsburg, Kansas; Bill Robertson from Arma, Kansas; and Frank Crespino from Pittsburg, Kansas. Lakeview Hall, a World War II navy barracks converted into a dormitory, is seen in the background.

The campus greenhouse in 1955 was located next to Whitesitt and Hartman halls.

Physical education majors hold a "bull session" outside the gymnasium in 1955.

Students visit the college bookstore in 1958.

Librarian John Harvey announced in November 1954 that Porter Library had added its 100,000th book to the collection. President Rees Hughes (left) and Rosemary Byrd, a student employee in the library, examine the book with Harvey.

Coach Carnie Smith and members of his 1954 football team visited a traveling circus camped north of Pittsburg. They posed for a photo with a diminutive gorilla that belonged to one of the animal trainers. Pictured, left to right, are Frank Crespino, LeRoy Simpson, Dale Bergsten, Smith, Burt Fowler, and Bob Hill.

Athletic trainer Al Ortolani talks to an injured official in 1955. A concerned coach, Carnie Smith, second from left, waits for play to resume.

Archery was a popular feature of "Recreational Activities," a course for women majoring in health and physical education during the 1950s. Five students take aim at their target on Brandenburg Field.

Mrs. Daphne Cross, assistant professor of education and supervisor of third-grade instruction at the Horace Mann Laboratory School, oversees four students learning to use the typewriter about 1953. These students were completing work in a course titled "Developing Skills in Self Expression."

Students from the Horace Mann Laboratory School are instructed in the workings of the traffic light in 1049. The lesson occurred at the corner of Broadway and Cleveland Streets; to the left is the Gorilla Inn, popular with college students before it closed in 1942.

Chapter Five

GREAT PERFORMANCES

*I felt confident. I was going to give everything I had. I felt that
I was going to win and jumped my best and hoped for the best.*

Kermit King

GREAT PERFORMANCES should not be attributed to luck; neither should they be called accidents. Rather, they are the result of talent, discipline, and commitment over a long time. They may arise from principle or a sense of duty, or we may discover they were rooted in hard work or artistic passion. Pittsburg State University has a sparkling legacy of alumni and faculty who have distinguished themselves in their chosen fields. The university also has a tradition of inviting the great and the near-great to the campus to inform, to entertain, and to inspire.

William Brandenburg moved the college toward academic and institutional respectability, and he sought to attract national attention during his presidency. Under his leadership, athletics and music were the two areas in which the institution most visibly excelled. In 1914 Brandenburg hired accomplished musician Walter McCray to be the new chairman of the Music Department. McCray inaugurated an annual Music Festival, the first event of its type in Kansas. In 1920 the festival expanded to include the annual Interstate High School Music Contest. Every year from 1915 to 1947, the week-long festival was highlighted by a production of Handel's *Messiah,* with over 150 voices, guest soloists, and full orchestral accompaniment conducted by McCray.

Guest performers through the years included, among many others, Amelita Galli-Curci, Percy Grainger, Jascha Heifetz, Ignace Jan Paderewski, and Ernestine Schumann-Heink. McCray's connections in the music world also made it possible for the campus to host composer Charles Wakefield Cadman, band leader John Philip Sousa, the Budapest String Quartet, the Robert Shaw Chorale, the Minneapolis Symphony Orchestra, and other outstanding performers.

In 1919 Brandenburg hired Garfield Weede to turn the school's athletic programs into powerhouses. Weede became coach of all men's sports until 1922, when he turned over basketball to John Lance. In 1929 Weede stopped coaching football but remained head of the Physical Education Department until 1947 and coach of track and field until 1957. Weede's track and field teams won fifteen conference championships between 1919 and 1957. Pittsburg also won more events in the prestigious meets at the University of Kansas, the University of Illinois, Drake University, and Butler University than any other college in the country.

Lance's tenure as head basketball coach included eight conference championships between 1922 and 1963, a forty-seven-game winning streak that spanned from 1929 to 1931, and his induction into three athletic

President William A. Brandenburg and several members of the faculty celebrated their completion of twenty or more years of service to the college in 1933. Left to right: David M. Bowen (1909), education; Margaret Coventry (1913), chemistry; James A. Yates (1907), physical sciences; James A. G. Shirk (1912), physics and mathematics; Brandenburg (1913), president; Andrew H. Whitesitt (1913), industrial education; Eulalia E. Roseberry (1907), geography; Odella Nation (1903), librarian; Oris Polk Dellinger (1909), biological sciences and dean; Belle Provorse (1913), business and financial secretary; and George W. Trout (1906), history and social sciences.

halls of fame. Lance was the fourth coach in the nation to earn over 600 career wins, and only the third with over 600 wins at the same college. The football program first gained national prominence after World War II under Coach Carnie Smith. The Gorillas won two NAIA national championships, and numerous players received All-American and All-Conference honors under his guidance. That football prominence has continued into the modern era with the most notable success coming under Chuck Broyles, who won an NCAA Division II national championship in 1991.

An amazing number of outstanding speakers and notable public figures were brought to the campus in the decades just after World War II. Poet W. H. Auden, critic Norman Cousins, bandleader Jimmy Dorsey, historian Bernard De Voto, artist Philip Evergood, activist Dick Gregory, novelist Elizabeth Bowen, inventor Buckminster Fuller, and musician Dizzy Gillespie

were among the dozens of guests in the 1950s and 1960s. In more recent years the campus has hosted individuals as diverse as FBI director Clarence Kelley, psychologist Ruth Westheimer, White House correspondent Helen Thomas, comic Steve Martin, Wal-Mart President H. Lee Scott, former U.S. Senator Robert Dole, and Kansas Governor Kathleen Sebelius.

Friends and alumni have long recognized that Pittsburg State University is a special place, but others realized that as well. Recent editions of *The Unbiased Guide to the 328 Most Interesting Colleges* have categorized Pittsburg State as a hidden treasure and placed it on a list of the twenty most underrated schools in the nation. National accreditations, scholarly publications, innovative research in polymers and green technologies, and excellence in athletics and academics ensure that the university will continue its tradition of great performances in the future.

ABOVE: The Komitas Russian String Quartet, organized at the University of Moscow in 1922, performed at Pittsburg State University in February 1963. The chairman of the Music Department, Millard Laing (far right), was on hand to welcome the quartet.

Theodore Sperry joined the Biology Department faculty at Pittsburg in 1946. Sperry's early work on the Curtis Prairie in Wisconsin with naturalist Aldo Leopold led to his international recognition as a pioneer of restoration ecology.

Historian Dudley Cornish
(right) presented a copy of
his award-winning book
The Sable Arm to librarian
John Harvey in 1956.
Cornish's seminal study
of black troops in the
Union Army, 1861–1865,
is still regarded as one of
the 100 best books on
the Civil War.

Georgia legislator Julian Bond visited the campus in 1969. A founding member of the Student Non-
violent Coordinating Committee and leader of the American civil rights movement, Bond in 1968
became the first African American to be proposed as a major party candidate for U.S. vice president
at the Democratic National Convention. The twenty-eight-year-old Bond quickly declined, however, citing the constitutional requirement that one must be thirty-five years of age to serve in that
office.

Consumer advocate Ralph Nader spoke to a campus
audience of 1,000 in October 1970 on the issue of
environmental hazards. In 1988 Nader made a second
visit to the campus to discuss "Reaganomics" and the
Washington power structure.

Debra Dene Barnes, a music major from Moran, Kansas,
became Miss America in 1968 while a student at the
college.

Father and son poets Louis Ginsberg and Allen Ginsberg were together for a 1972 appearance on campus. They spent three days visiting sites in Pittsburg and southeast Kansas.

Shirley Christian, a 1960 Pittsburg journalism graduate, won the 1980 Pulitzer Prize for Foreign Reporting for her articles from El Salvador and Guatemala that appeared in the *Miami Herald*. In this photograph Christian interviews Lt. Col. Sigifredo Ochoa in El Salvador.

James Tate graduated from Pittsburg with a degree in English in 1965. In 1992 he won the Pulitzer Prize for Poetry for his work *Selected Poems.* In 1994 Tate received the National Book Award for *Worshipful Company of Fletchers.* He was a guest reader on campus in 1969 for a celebration of the life of Margaret Haughawout, an early Pittsburg teacher and poet. At the celebration are (left to right) Joseph Gorentz, Sherry Newell, Tate, Charles Cagle, Gene DeGruson, and Ivan Hentschel.

The Pittsburg State University ROTC team was tops in the nation at a Ranger Challenge meet held at the University of Kansas in November 1997. During the competition, Sean Weeks received help to hook himself onto the one-rope bridge.

The Students in Free Enterprise chapter from Pittsburg State University was named international champion at the 1998 Hallmark Cards/Students in Free Enterprise (SIFE) Exposition and Career Opportunity Fair in Kansas City, Missouri. Pittsburg State was tops among ninety SIFE chapters in the competition.

The first undefeated wrestling team champions of the Kansas Intercollegiate Athletic Conference in 1926 were from Pittsburg. Standing, left to right: Coach George Walker, Frank Campbell, and Luther Otis Brickey. Seated, left to right: Robert Brickey, George Allen, and Curt John Reimer.

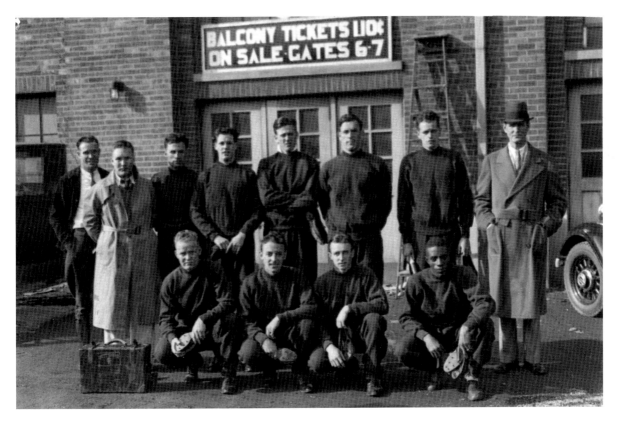

Garfield Weede's track team won the Knute Rockne Trophy at the Central Conference track meet at Marquette University, Milwaukee, Wisconsin, on June 2, 1933. Back row, left to right: Duncan, Lester Needham, John W. Bell, Vinson Tingley, Fred Stambach, Ralph Russell, Richard Terwilliger, and Weede. Front row: Abner Bidwell, Elton Brown, Dale Smith, and Lawrence Swisher. Weede wrote, it was "without a doubt, the greatest victory for a K.S.T.C. team because of the caliber of the competition." Pittsburg's competition at the meet included athletes from Butler, Marquette, Notre Dame, Wisconsin, Michigan State, and Loyola universities.

Joe Winchester breaks the tape as Pittsburg sets a record for the two-mile relay in the college division at the eighth annual University of Kansas Relays in Lawrence in 1930. The record time of 8:02:04 was set by Joy Cullison, Kermit Sandusky, James Waner, and Winchester.

Pittsburg hosted the Central Intercollegiate Conference track and field championships in 1954. That year Pittsburg won its second consecutive title and its fifteenth conference championship since the conference was inaugurated in 1928.

Track and field trophies on display in 1938. The track and field teams of Coach Garfield Weede won ten consecutive conference championships before the 1938 season.

1931
CENTRAL CONFERENCE CHAMPIONS

GARDNER LANCE SCHMIDT WACHTER JACK VANEK LEWIS

KAHLER McCLURE JOHNSON KINCAID RATZLAFF HACKWORTH

The 1931 Central Conference basketball champions ended their season with a record of 21–0 and the seventh conference championship in the preceding nine seasons for Pittsburg. This team was part of a forty-seven-game winning streak, from March 1929 to January 1931. The streak ended when the Gorillas lost 20–18 to a Maryville (Missouri) Teachers College squad coached by Henry Iba. Ironically, the year before, the Gorilla squad had ended Maryville's forty-one-game winning streak.

John Foster Lance was named NAIA coach of the year in 1956. His tenure as head basketball coach was highlighted by 8 conference championships and 644 career victories.

Pittsburg defeated Hillsdale College from Michigan in the Holiday Bowl in St. Petersburg, Florida, by a score of 27–26 to become NAIA national football champions in 1957. Red Grange and Chip Bolin called the game on national television for CBS.

The NAIA national football championship team of 1961. Coach Carnie Smith was voted national coach of the year after the 12–7 victory over the College of McMinnville.

Coaches Joe Murphy and Carnie Smith prepare for the national title game at the Camellia Bowl in Sacramento, California, December 9, 1961.

Coach Chuck Broyles holds up the NCAA Division II national football trophy after the Gorillas' 23–6 victory over Jacksonville State on December 14, 1991.

111

Kermit King became national AAU and NCAA broad-jump champion in the spring of 1937. As a member of the All-American track and field team in 1937, he toured Japan and Asia. King received his bachelor's degree in 1936 and his master's degree from Pittsburg in 1937. In 1947 he earned a doctorate from the University of California. King later worked for the U.S. State Department and served as the president of the Liberian National University in the 1950s.

Christie Allen was twice a GTE Academic All-American, while winning eight NCAA Division II championships in cross-country, indoor track and field, and outdoor track and field. She also won eleven All-American awards. Allen became the first Division II athlete to win back-to-back triple crowns—national championships in cross-country, indoor track, and outdoor track—during her junior and senior seasons.

Chapter Six

KANSAS STATE COLLEGE OF PITTSBURG, 1959–1977

The development of the desire to know and the teaching of effective methods of independent study are the most valuable things we can give our students.

George Budd

LEONARD H. AXE, president from 1957 to 1965, insisted on a focus for the Kansas State Teachers College different from that promoted by presidents Rees Hughes and William Brandenburg. Axe's academic and professional background in business administration prompted and directed the changed focus. Heads of academic departments became chairmen and Axe created three new positions: graduate dean, dean of administration, and dean of instruction. The curriculum was expanded again to allow for a greater variety of degree options and to place a greater emphasis on the liberal arts. Taken together, the administrative and curricular changes Axe promoted were the final steps in the college's transformation from teachers' college to Kansas State College of Pittsburg in 1959. Axe also stressed that modern students needed to assume responsibility for themselves and for their education. A *Collegio* editorial noted on September 26, 1957, that the program President Axe "advocated . . . is an extremely liberal and modern concept of education. It will prove shocking to some, including students and faculty alike,

while to others it may well be the refreshing breath of scholastic encouragement and insistence upon the development of individual responsibility which has been long-missing from the campus."

Enrollment increased 300 percent during the two decades after World War II, drawing attention to a lack of adequate physical facilities at the college. An addition of seven dormitories helped the housing shortage, and the completion of the Russ Hall annex partially satisfied the need for more classroom space. Further expansions planned in the 1950s, however, were not realized until the following decade. In 1962 Hughes Hall opened as a classroom building for education and psychology. Yates Hall was dedicated in 1964 for use by the Mathematics and Physics departments. The English, Communications, and Foreign Language departments moved into the new Grubbs Hall in 1968. Together, these three buildings further alleviated the shortage of classroom space. The construction of new facilities made it necessary to extend the campus to the east. The completion of the Garfield Weede Physical Education Building in 1971

"Hanging out" with good friends as it was done in 1959.

and the dedication of the McPherson Nurse Education Building in 1977 were among the first examples of the campus's physical expansion outside the traditional boundaries of the central campus Oval.

In August 1962 the campus learned of the death of the college's founder and first administrator, Russell S. Russ. He died at his home in Muskogee, Oklahoma, at the age of 102. Russ was remembered for establishing the college and leading the fight for separation of the Pittsburg school from Emporia. For that leadership Russ was dismissed as the chief administrator in 1911—an action generally credited by campus historians to Governor Walter R. Stubbs, who bowed to political pressure and ignored Russ's pioneering efforts. Russ entered the banking and loan business in Pittsburg after his dismissal and retired in 1935. When he turned 100 in 1960, Russ was asked what advice he had to give to the students and alumni of the Kansas

State College. "Don't look for trouble," he said. "It will come soon enough. And when it does, do the best you can and forget it. Make an effort to remember the pleasant things in your life; forget the unpleasant. You'll be an unhappy old grouch if you don't."

The school Russ started in 1903 with fifty-four students reached a new high in 1962 with over 3,900 students. In that same year, 1962, Carnie Smith was elected president of the NAIA Coaches Association, and the campus celebrated the selection of international student Hedy Hashimoto as homecoming queen. The next year John Lance concluded his forty-first season as head basketball coach at the college with a total of 644 career victories. Former President Rees Hughes was named "Kansan of the Year" in 1963. During that time, many students on campus read a mystery novel, *The Irrepressible Peccadillo,* written by Fletcher Flora, a Pittsburg alum from the class of

Governor George Docking signed the bill that officially changed Kansas State Teachers College to Kansas State College of Pittsburg on March 12, 1959. In this photograph Docking reviews the signed document with his secretary before sending it along to Pittsburg.

1938 who won the Cock Robin Mystery Award for his 1960 novel, *The Killing Cousins.* In 1963 the new dean of women, Pat Patterson, helped to relax the female dress code on campus. Long dresses were no longer de rigueur on campus. "Bermuda shorts, jamaicas, and slacks," according to the student handbook, "will be allowed in the Library, Gorilla Den, and Gorilla Grill after 5 P.M. on weekdays and all day on weekends except for Sunday.... Jeans, levis, shorts, and short shorts," however, "may be worn only on the way to the tennis courts." Ratted hairdos were the vogue nationally, but *Collegio* columnist Glenda Richardson bemoaned the fact that "the coeds at KSC have evidently not been reading their fashion magazines faithfully" since "hairdos on campus are definitely bouffant" (August 28, 1962).

Axe left the presidency in 1965 and was replaced by George Budd, who came to the campus with vast experience in higher education administration, including fourteen years as president of St. Cloud College in Minnesota. Budd quickly revised the college's administrative structure so it more resembled a university, perhaps anticipating another name change that was still more than a decade in the future. Under Budd's leadership, Willis L. Tompkins, dean of the college since 1964, filled the new position of academic vice president. When Tompkins left to become president of Missouri Valley College in July 1968, J. D. Haggard replaced Alvin Proctor as graduate dean and Proctor was named academic vice president. C. Ray Baird was appointed to the executive vice president position that Proctor had held since its inception in 1966. The three schools of Arts and Sciences, Education, and Technology were created, along with twenty-one academic departments, to further the administrative changes. It was 1975 before the creation of a separate School of Business and Economics completed the reorganization.

Enrollment reached another all-time high in 1968, with 5,914 full-time students, before declining slightly in the early 1970s. Unrest over civil rights, the Vietnam War, and women's rights affected the Pittsburg campus, as it did on every other campus in the nation. Conflicts between the Budd administration and the student leadership of the campus newspaper led to the dismissal or resignation of several student journalists. The faculty successfully demanded a greater level of input in decision-making and governance through the Faculty Senate and through participation on curricula, tenure, and promotion committees. The faculty also installed a union bargaining unit, the first of its kind on any college or university campus in Kansas. Federal mandates relating to affirmative action also reshaped the institution's athletic programs, faculty activities, and long-range mission during the lively decade of the 1970s.

Kansas State College of Pittsburg garnered national attention in several ways between 1959 and 1977. The college earned national and professional academic accreditations in teacher education, chemistry, and music. In 1961 the football team won its second NAIA national championship. In September 1964, incoming freshman Linda Greer appeared on the cover of *Look* magazine. Greer, from Labette County, Kansas, was

Three great Pittsburg coaches were inducted into the Helms Athletic Foundation Hall of Fame in Los Angeles for their accomplishments in football, track and field, and basketball. Left to right: Carnie Smith, Garfield Weede, and John Lance. Smith came to the college in 1949 as head football coach and led the Gorillas to NAIA national titles in 1957 and 1961. Weede came to Pittsburg State in 1919 as the athletic director, head of the Physical Education Department, and coach of all men's sports. His greatest coaching success was in track and field, where he won fifteen conference championships. Lance graduated from the State Manual Training Normal in 1918 and returned in 1922 as head coach of men's basketball. He was the fourth coach in the nation to reach over 600 career victories. In the early 1930s his team had a winning streak of forty-seven games and he was named NAIA coach of the year in 1956.

featured in an article that focused on the national freshman class of 1964 that was 20 percent bigger than the previous year's and, according to *Look* editors, "better prepared than ever." Four years later, Debra Dene Barnes, a music major from Moran, Kansas, would represent KSCP and the nation as Miss America for 1968. Nationally prominent speakers also drew attention to the campus during these years. Included were appearances by beat poet Allen Ginsberg, politician Julian Bond, consumer advocate Ralph Nader, psychologist Joyce Brothers, foreign affairs specialist

J. William Fulbright, politicians Shirley Chisholm and George McGovern, and feminist Betty Friedan.

In his tenth year as president, Budd challenged the 1975 graduates of KSCP to be prepared to deal with the problems of their day. "It is time," he said, "we took a look at ourselves and our world, that we determine the dimensions of the problem and lay down a plan for correcting some of the errors and faults. We seem to be unable to understand that more than a game plan has gone wrong." Some of the problems Budd alluded to were the fall of South Vietnam after

Former President Rees Hughes (left) and President Leonard Axe (center) visit Russell S. Russ on his 100th birthday on February 9, 1960. Russ was the college's founder and first principal, from 1903 to 1911. Movies and photographs of the event were broadcast on local television stations that evening.

thirty years of conflict, the Watergate scandal and subsequent resignation of President Richard Nixon, soaring inflation, high gas prices, and a deepening economic recession.

On many occasions, Budd had followed his own advice to "get involved." In May 1970, for example, Budd was one of thirty-seven college presidents to send an open telegram to Nixon inviting a discussion of the Cambodian situation, Kent State, and the alienation of the youth in America. Students in the 1970s were involved in everything from transcendental meditation and belly dancing to spades tournaments and a political campaign to save the tallgrass prairie in Kansas. The *Kanza* staff also collected over 6,000 signatures on a petition demanding a safer U.S. Highway 69, to save the lives of students traveling north of Pitts-

burg. The first year of mandated intercollegiate athletic competition for women was 1974, and the student newspaper reported that apparently no money was available for women's athletics. But teams for volleyball, basketball, and softball were organized anyway, compiling records of 8–12, 0–10, and 12–5, respectively.

The college, higher education, and the nation experienced tremendous changes between 1959 and 1977. Change, whether mandated, unexpected, or directed, was inevitable. As the college approached its seventy-fifth anniversary, in 1977 another name change—this time to Pittsburg State University—symbolized the institution's continuing maturation. Beginning that year, new leadership would be challenged to direct and control a vibrant university focused on even greater opportunities.

Members of the newly organized Kip Club practice their synchronized swimming programs in February 1960. Members of the club gave exhibitions at local swim meets throughout the spring semester.

Steady growth in the student population led to a continual campus housing shortage. In 1961 several women students were housed at the Hotel Besse in downtown Pittsburg, and they commuted to and from campus by bus.

OPPOSITE: The college's Young Democrats club traveled thirty miles to Joplin, Missouri, to see presidential candidate John F. Kennedy in 1960. College photographer Chuck Thomas snapped this close-up of Kennedy.

Automotive students host an open house in Hartman Hall in April 1961.

Theater students and volunteer members of the Pittsburg Jaycee Jaynes help prepare for Tent-by-the-Lake in the summer of 1963. The annual outdoor summer theater performances began in 1959, and four productions of *The Fantasticks, Ring Round the Moon, The Seven Year Itch,* and *Finian's Rainbow* were planned for the 1963 season.

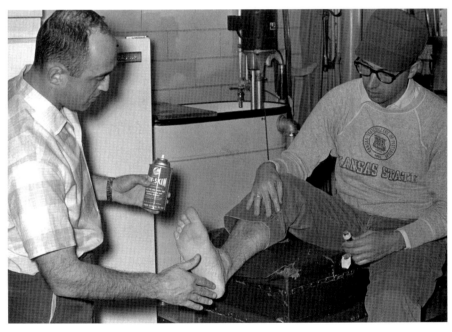

In 1963 professor Millard Laing, chairman of the Music Department, introduced students to Tchaikovsky and other classic composers in his course "Music Appreciation."

Athletic trainer Al Ortolani applies Tuf-Skin to Charles Brady's foot in February 1963. Brady, a Spanish teacher at College High School, planned to walk the round trip from Pittsburg to Fort Scott, Kansas, in one day. Leaving with thirteen other walkers at 4:30 A.M., Brady, Larry Brillhart, and Harold Wilson finished the 51-mile route in seventeen and a half hours. Freshman Steve Bolton walked 50 miles but his feet were too blistered to finish the last mile. Ortolani played football at the college from 1948 to 1951, when an injury ended his career. He became an assistant athletic trainer for the team and was promoted to head athletic trainer at the college in 1955. Before retiring in 1995, Ortolani had been selected to be an Olympic trainer four times.

The Collegiates, a college choral group, traveled to Topeka during the winter break in 1963 to sing for the Kansas House of Representatives. The invitation came from state Representative Rees Hughes, the college's president emeritus.

"All present and accounted for, sir!" ROTC cadets board a bus headed for a field exercise at Camp Crowder, Missouri, in 1964.

The Pittsburg community attends a memorial observance for President John F. Kennedy held on the campus Oval on November 25, 1963. Cadets from the college's ROTC program conducted the service on the national day of mourning.

Members of Sigma Sigma Sigma, a national education sorority, host a picnic in 1964. The Chi chapter of the sorority was established at Pittsburg State University in 1922.

Students in the Math Department work out their problems in 1964.

Pi Kappa Alpha fraternity members work on house decorations for homecoming in 1963. Left to right: Mike Doherty, Gary Nicklaus, and Ron Johnson. Arsonists were blamed for setting fire to Alpha Sigma Alpha house decorations and a residence hall float just before that year's parade.

The homecoming dance in 1965 featured music by the Fendermen and the entertainment included this unidentified go-go dancer.

Campus police began using motorcycles
to patrol the college in 1965.

John Laws, a senior from Grand-
view, Missouri, dedicated the
Operation Viet Nam campaign
to his brother, Billy Laws, a member of the Marine Corps killed in
action in the fall of 1966. The campaign obtained over 1,500 signatures on a Christmas card fifty feet
in length and raised $850 in dona-
tions to purchase canned fruit for
American soldiers in Vietnam.
Tau Kappa Epsilon sponsored
the project and forwarded the
card and funds to K Company,
Third Battalion, Fourth Marine
Regiment.

ABOVE: Johnny Bennett (shown in top photo with Colombian children), a senior from Baxter Springs, Kansas, was one of several students involved with the Peace Corps in 1961, serving in Colombia.

OPPOSITE: Faculty members of the Art Department arranged this photo op in 1968. Left to right: Laurence Wooster, Frank Machek, Marjorie Schick, Alex Barde, Harry Krug, Reed Schmickle, and Robert Blunk.

Members of the college's Black Student Movement pay tribute to the late Dr. Martin Luther King Jr. in a memorial march on April 9, 1968. All afternoon classes at the college were dismissed and approximately 200 marchers were escorted through downtown Pittsburg by city police officers and the Kansas Highway Patrol.

Groundbreaking ceremonies for the Garfield Weede Physical Education Building were held in 1969. Participants included (left to right) John Lance, Bill Dickey, Prentice Gudgen, Dorothy Weede Bethel, Garfield Weede, and George Budd.

Members of campus sororities were invited to compete in the sixth annual Sigma Chi "Derby Days" in 1971, originated in 1930 by the Sigma Chi fraternity at the University of California.

FAR LEFT AND LEFT: Members of the Black Student Movement protest the Miss Pitt State contest in April 1970 after the Student Senate rejected a request for an allocation from the student activity fee to finance a separate Miss Black Pitt State pageant.

Sophomore Brenda Wiedner learns that she has just been selected Kanza Queen for 1971. Left to right: Jill Swan, Riva Coleman, Wiedner, Becky Winter, and Susan Brookshier.

Members of the fledgling women's liberation movement at the college distribute pamphlets and picket outside the Miss Pitt State pageant in 1972. The protestors believed such traditional beauty pageants undermined their struggle to achieve women's equality.

John Kerry, antiwar activist
and military veteran, discusses
the Vietnam War with a
reporter during a 1973 visit
to the Pittsburg campus.

Students in the college's Theater Department production of *The Serpent* pose for a publicity shot in 1973. The production won at the district level of the American Theater Association college production competition and advanced to the regional competition, held in Lawrence, Kansas, in 1974. The improvisational performance relating to the assassinations of John F. Kennedy and Martin Luther King Jr. was written by Jean-Claude van Itallie. The performance won an award of merit at the regional level.

Cover design by
Aaron Smith & Lorenzo Morris

RIGHT: An advertisement for Black Heritage Week activities in 1974. The week's events included an exhibition of African sculpture, a jazz concert, a soul food dinner, a performance by the Black Exodus dance troupe from Kansas City, and a reading by poet Don L. Lee.

BELOW: Biological science students put the college's laboratory equipment to good use.

Graduating nurses participate in the traditional pinning ceremony in McCray Hall auditorium, circa 1976. The Kansas Board of Regents authorized a four-year nursing program for the college in the spring of 1970. This coincided with the completion of a new Mt. Carmel Hospital in Pittsburg and the closing of the Mt. Carmel School of Nursing, which had operated since before World War II. One of the most significant enhancements of the nursing program came in September 1977 with the dedication of the McPherson Nurse Education Building, a gift from the estates of four members of the McPherson family who were all graduates of the college.

RIGHT: At the height of the Vietnam War, Pittsburg coeds (left to right) Mary Helen Blood, Pamela Greenfield, Tana Garrett, Linda Abraham, and Shirley Benedict receive a tour of Richards-Gebaur Air Force Base near Kansas City from recruiting officer Dick Boman in 1968.

Behind the scenes at Porter Library, cataloger Helen Land (center) was known for her unapproved smoking and for her prodigious amounts of work—even taking home copies of the *Library of Congress Subject Headings* to work through the evenings.

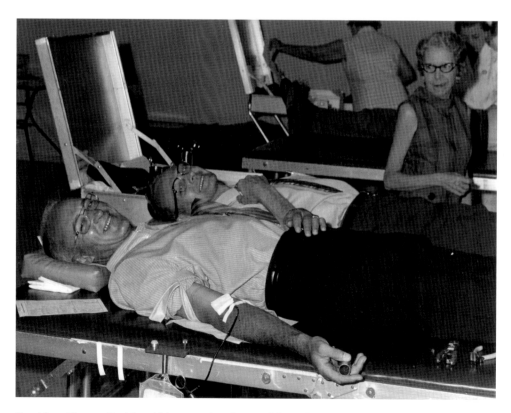

President George Budd and his executive vice president, C. Ray Baird, donate to a good cause.

President Leonard Axe talks it over with the team on the sideline.

Professor Don Milliken discusses learning methods of classroom education in the sciences for future teachers, circa 1958.

Physical plant and custodial employees, circa 1975.

Overcrowding in Porter Library was a problem as student enrollments skyrocketed in the 1950s and 1960s. Plans for new library facilities were on the drawing board for over fifteen years before the Axe Library was opened in 1979.

Students who traveled to and from college on U.S. Highway 69 north of Pittsburg will never forget its reputation as a killer. The editors of the 1974 *Kanza* noted that eleven people had died on the highway between Pittsburg and Fort Scott over the previous six years.

Students are introduced to the operation of a Linotype machine in the Printing Department.

Professor Edwin Harbeston of the Department of Curriculum and Instruction takes tea with Lori Parsons in 1964. Harbeston's students in his class on childhood psychology were keen observers of the interaction between the professor and his guest.

Chapter Seven

THE CAMPUS

*We left here in a cloud of dust with a portfolio under my arm
and a dream to be an artist.*

Joe Beeler

THE ORIGINAL CAMPUS of 17 acres, purchased in 1905, was located on the southern boundary of Pittsburg. The university has since expanded to more than 200 acres while the city has grown up around it. The first building on the new campus, Russ Hall, opened in January 1909, and more than thirty major buildings now mark the university's landscape. Most of these buildings, as well as other university facilities and sites, are named for people significant in the university's history, American higher education, or the state of Kansas.

When William Aaron Brandenburg celebrated his twenty-fifth anniversary as president of the college in 1938, faculty member Irma Gene Nevins paid him tribute by quoting Ralph Waldo Emerson's statement that "an institution is the lengthened shadow of one man." Besides contributing to the college's educational vision, academic rank, and leadership, Nevins noted, Brandenburg also determined in large part the physical design of the campus. It was at Brandenburg's request that the Board of Administration employed the firm of Hare and Hare of Kansas City, Missouri, to draw up plans for future buildings and campus development. The board adopted the plans in the summer of 1917, and the resulting arrangement of

the principal campus buildings around the central Oval still dominates the campus landscape today. Sixteen buildings, including the athletic stadium, were part of that campus plan by 1940, when Brandenburg's twenty-seven-year tenure as president ended.

The campus's physical facilities proved inadequate after World War II, however, as the enrollment increased 300 percent between 1945 and 1965. A second significant campus expansion began with the construction of seven dormitory buildings after 1953. This upset the quaint, symmetrical order maintained by similar buildings of approximate size facing each other around the Oval. Trout, Tanner, Bowen, and Shirk residence halls were constructed on the northeast corner of the campus, while Mitchell, Nation, and Dellinger residence halls were built on the southwest corner. It was not long before the campus also began to spread eastward, with the completion of Timmons Chapel (1966), Weede Gymnasium (1972), McPherson Hall (1977), and Axe Library (1979).

One of the most significant buildings in the early years, Carney Hall and Auditorium, was vacated in November 1978 due to structural deterioration and was razed in 1980. A new science building, Heckert-Wells Hall, was dedicated on the Carney Hall site in

A panorama of the campus taken in the summer of 1924. Visible from left to right are the geology building, now part of the Overman Student Center; the gymnasium; Carney Hall; the cafeteria, later rededicated as Chandler Hall; the industrial arts building, now Whitesitt Hall; and Willard Hall.

1984. Heckert-Wells Hall and the renovation of the stadium in 1989 were the primary construction projects on campus during the 1980s. Significant projects since that time have included the Gene Bicknell Sports Complex (1995), the Kansas Technology Center (1997), the renovation of Horace Mann School (2000), the renovation of Russ Hall (2001), additions to Carnie Smith Stadium (2001 and 2006), the Family and Consumer Sciences Building (2004), the Veterans Memorial Amphitheater (2004), the Tyler Research Center (2007), and the Student Recreation Center/ National Guard Armory (2008).

The permanent display of art on the Pittsburg campus began with the organization of the College Art Club in 1921. The club's founders included Helen Waskey, who executed the first image of the Gorilla mascot, and Waylande Gregory, later famous for his ceramics and sculptures made for the Cowan Art Pottery Studio of Ohio and the Cranbrook Academy of Art in New Jersey. Birger Sandzen, the best-known Kansas landscape artist, was one of numerous artists who held exhibitions on the campus in the 1930s and 1940s. The university owns several of his valuable

works. Most prominently, two Sandzen oil paintings have hung in the foyer of McCray Hall since 1945. Several more recent works by Joe Beeler, a founding member of the Cowboy Artists of America and a 1957 graduate of Pittsburg State University, also grace the campus. Since 2000 the university administration has emphasized commissioning and acquiring significant pieces of outdoor art, including a bronze sculpture by Beeler titled *Night Song*.

Visitors frequently remark on the beauty of the campus and the variety of its aesthetic and architectural features. That beauty is due largely to the talent and dedication of the physical plant employees who maintain the campus and all its features. A closer look reveals that in addition to its physical attributes, the campus has over 7,000 students, over 300 faculty members, theater and choral groups, a student-run newspaper, a National Public Radio affiliate station, over 140 student organizations and clubs, national sororities and fraternities, national-caliber athletics, and numerous educational and recreational opportunities.

An aerial view of the campus taken in 1932 prominently features the Oval. The geology building survives as part of the Overman Student Center, but the gymnasium; the science building, known as Carney Hall; the cafeteria, known as Chandler Hall; and the Army barracks from World War I are no longer a part of the campus.

A general assembly of the faculty and students gathered for this photograph in the original Russ Hall auditorium in 1913. Principal George Edmund Myers, seated in the front row, center, fourth from the right, would be dismissed from his position just days later as a result of the administrative separation of the Pittsburg and Emporia normal schools.

Classes met in Whitesitt Hall, in tents, and in other temporary quarters after the Russ Hall fire. The entire summer school course of 1914 was completed, however, and not a single student withdrew from the school after the fire.

Before and after views of the walk from Broadway to the front of Russ Hall in the summer of 1914. These images were made just days before and one day after the tragic fire of June 30.

In 1913 the industrial arts building was completed, becoming the second classroom building on the campus. In 1964 the building was rededicated as Whitesitt Hall to honor Andrew H. Whitesitt, head of the Woodworking Department for many years.

OPPOSITE: The southeast corner of Russ Hall after the 1914 fire that claimed the life of Rex Tanner, principal of the public high school in Weir, Kansas. Tanner was attending the college's summer session to earn the final credits for his bachelor's degree. He was assisting firemen when an electric line fell, startling a pair of fire horses standing nearby. As Tanner attempted to quiet the horses he came in contact with the live wire and was fatally burned.

When Carney Hall, also known as Science Hall, was completed in 1919 it housed the departments of Home Economics, Chemical and Physical Sciences, Biology, and Agriculture. The building was named for Thomas Carney, the second governor of Kansas.

The gymnasium in 1957. Constructed in 1922, it served the campus until 1971, when it was replaced by the Garfield W. Weede Physical Education Building.

The first cafeteria building was completed in 1922. In 1951 it was renovated for the Home Economics Department and in 1964 was rededicated as Chandler Hall to honor the first director of the department, Sarah Chandler Hartsock. Chandler Hall was slated for renovation in 2001 but extensive structural damage led instead to its demolition in 2002. The new Family and Consumer Sciences Building was completed on the same site and dedicated in April 2004.

Students, faculty, alumni, and friends of the college initiated a drive for a new athletic field and stadium in 1922. The initial $60,000 to pay for the construction came from contributions from 1,484 faculty members, students, and alumni plus 332 Pittsburg citizens. When it was completed in 1924, the stadium was recognized as the first concrete stadium in the United States to be erected on the campus of a teachers' college.

In 1927 the first library building was completed and named for Ebenezer Porter, the state senator from Pittsburg who was instrumental in the university's founding and early appropriations.

The main reading room on the second floor of Porter Library as it appeared in 1932.

The lobby of McCray Hall has hosted numerous receptions and gatherings for the Music Department and the campus since it opened in 1929. The decorative and acoustical tiles in McCray Hall came from the Rookwood Pottery Company.

This aerial photograph of the campus taken about 1938 includes a view of the college lake before it was expanded and the stadium before the east bleachers were completed in 1940.

The southern exposure of McCray Hall in 1965.

The campus heating plant, shown here in 1913, is now the third oldest surviving building on the campus.

Summer school students in 1922 pose in front of Carney, Chandler, and Whitesitt halls.

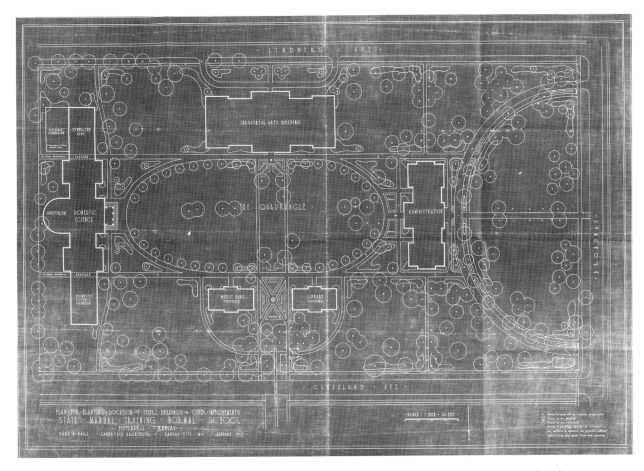

A blueprint of the campus design proposed by Kansas City architectural firm Hare and Hare in 1917. The plan was conceived at the request of President William Brandenburg.

An aerial view of the
campus circa 1970.

The Brooker Memorial Sundial was dedicated in March 2000 to honor George Ray
Brooker, professor of automotive technology from 1959 to 1992. The sundial is both
a work of art and a technological marvel. It stands nearly twelve feet high and is
constructed of two blocks of Minnesota granite weighing 4,200 pounds and 3,000
pounds. The sundial also contains nearly 500 pounds of stainless steel.

The Benelli Memorial Clock, for many years a fixture in downtown Pittsburg, was donated to the university by the Benelli family and dedicated on October 26, 2002, in memory of Martin J. "Bud" Benelli Sr., a longtime supporter of the university.

In the spring of 2000 the Student Government Association dedicated the water fountain "Cadence" to the students of Pittsburg State University. The copper fountain, located on Willard Plaza, was designed by artist Jon Havener.

Mark Switlik, a 1979 Pittsburg graduate, completed the Centennial Mural in 2004. The 43-by-41-foot mural is painted on the north end of Nation Hall. Among the twenty-one images are Russ Hall after the 1914 fire, decorative tiles from McCray Hall, and the Waylande Gregory relief that decorates the football stadium.

Two bronze sculptures, *Secure the Blessings of Liberty* and *Peace and Tranquility,* by Constance Ann Ernatt were installed at the Veterans Memorial Amphitheater in 2004.

The official seal of Pittsburg State University incorporates elements of historic Russ Hall and identifies the university's earlier names. The seal also identifies the institution's abiding objectives of research, instruction, and service.

Rising enrollment sometimes makes it difficult for students to find housing. Crimson Village, a recent university development in the east campus area, is one of the innovative projects designed to alleviate the housing shortage. Formerly known as Bonita Terrace Apartments, the complex was originally constructed in 1980 and purchased by the City of Pittsburg in 2003. The city then entered into an agreement with the university to renovate and operate the complex. The twenty duplex units, sitting on six acres on East Ford Street, were renovated primarily by members of the Pittsburg State University physical plant staff.

The statue of the gorilla mascot, located near the Overman Student Center, was a gift from the 1965 senior class. The statue was designed by Larry Wooster, a member of the Art Department faculty.

Chapter Eight

PITTSBURG STATE UNIVERSITY,
1977–2004

The University has always endeavored to put students first.
It is who we are and it is what we do best.

Dr. Tom Bryant

WITH THE ACQUISITION of university status in 1977 came an expanded vision of the roles to be played by Pittsburg State University administrators, faculty, students, staff, and alumni. Governor Robert Bennett came to the campus in 1977 to congratulate the new president, James Appleberry, on his position and the university on its new status. Bennett also applauded the students for their lobbying efforts of the legislature on behalf of unionizing the university faculty. Tom Hemmens of the English Department and Mary Roberts of the Speech Communication Department published an introduction to a new critical edition of Thomas Paine's *Common Sense.* Alumnus Dale Leibach returned to campus to discuss his job as press aide to President Jimmy Carter. The university's first Creative Writing Festival honored alum James Tate, a 1965 graduate who would win the Pulitzer Prize for Poetry in 1992. "Tate's presence here," noted former English professor Dr. Michael Heffernan in *Collegio,* April 26, 1978, "illustrates the purpose of this festival: namely, that though Southeast Kansas is undeniably a cultural backwater well out of the mainstream of the big pub-

lishing houses and literary magazines, it has as much a right as any other place for poetry. 'Backwater' does not imply stagnation."

In 1978 Eva Jessye, a native of Coffeyville, Kansas, and the original choral director for George Gershwin's Broadway production of *Porgy and Bess,* became an artist-in-residence on the campus. Jessye, who had toured the world with her choir for over fifty years, directed a production of her own folk oratorio, *Paradise Lost and Regained,* as part of the university's seventy-fifth anniversary celebration. A new $3.6 million library opened in August 1979, replacing the outdated Porter Library, which had served the campus since 1927. In 1980 Carolann Martin of the Music Department became the first American woman to win the National Adult Conducting Competition. That same year librarian Gene DeGruson would launch an award-winning, small-press quarterly called the *Little Balkans Review.* In 1981 Shirley Christian, a 1960 graduate, received the Pulitzer Prize for International Reporting for a series of articles on El Salvador and Guatemala that appeared in the *Miami Herald.* Christian, later a correspondent for the *New York Times,*

Members of the women's softball team prepare for their first game in the KAIAW state tournament in 1978.

An all-school toga party at the Tower in November 1978 featured a John Belushi look-alike contest. Music was provided by Otis Day and the Knights, who had appeared in the popular Belushi film *Animal House*.

was the first Kansan to win a Pulitzer Prize since William Allen White in 1923. In 1982 Pittsburg State graphic designer and illustrator Rod Dutton was commissioned to design the official commemorative medallion for that year's World's Fair.

In 1983 the Kansas Board of Regents made drastic cuts to the university's budget and proposed a 10 percent tuition increase. In-state undergraduate tuition raised from $365 per semester to $421 in the fall of 1983. The budget cuts no doubt accounted for the virtual disappearance of nationally known speakers on

the campus during the mid-1980s. Even commencement was eventually affected, for the keynote speaker in 1983 was not a world-famous writer, entrepreneur, or government official, but the president of the university, Appleberry, who days earlier had announced his resignation.

In the face of financial challenges in the 1980s, the university could still look back to some of its past strengths and forward to a bright future. A new science building that cost nearly $6 million was dedicated and named for two longtime faculty members, L. C. Heckert and J. Ralph Wells. The student union was renamed the Overman Student Center in honor of Jack Overman, the center's director since 1951. Al Ortolani, head athletic trainer for twenty-eight years, became the first trainer in the nation to be inducted into the NAIA Hall of Fame. The gymnasium in the Garfield Weede Physical Education building was renamed the John Lance Arena to honor the longtime basketball coach. Carnie Smith was also honored when the football stadium was renovated and renamed for him in 1989.

One Pitt State student who did not have "disco fever" in 1978. Five local venues—Schoolhouse Disco, Blue Barn Disco, the Matador Lounge, Paw Paws Disco, and Good Times Disco—all had closed their doors or switched to New Wave and soft rock music by 1980.

Gorilla athletics also returned to national prominence in the 1980s. Dennis Franchione was named head football coach in December 1984 and compiled a record of 30 wins and 4 losses during his three seasons. In 1987 the Gorillas captured the school's 400th all-time football win in a victory over Washburn University and the 1987 team set an all-time NAIA single-season team rushing record of 3,946 yards. In 1989 Pittsburg State moved from NAIA athletic competition to NCAA Division II status. Chuck Broyles was named head football coach in 1989 when Franchione left for another position. Two seasons later the Gorillas captured the 1991 Division II national championship in football with a 23–6 victory over Jacksonville State. In that same year Pittsburg receiver Ronnie West won the Harlon Hill Trophy honoring the top player in Division II. Two years later, in 1993, Christie Allen, a two-time GTE Academic All-American, completed her athletic career at Pittsburg State after winning eight Division II championships and eleven All-American awards in track and field and cross-country.

Many of the physical changes to the campus in recent years were initiated in 1986 when President Donald W. Wilson and Pittsburg State University Foundation officials announced the first major fundraising campaign in the university's history. The Campaign for Distinction concluded in 1990, having surpassed its goal of raising $9.8 million. In 1988 the KRPS-FM radio station was established on campus as an affiliate of National Public Radio. In spring 1989, work on the Prentice Gudgen track was completed and construction of the August and Helen Rua press box in Carnie Smith Stadium was under way. In 1990 the university received verbal confirmation from U.S. Senator Robert Dole that $6 million was appropriated for expanding the technology program and facilities. That project culminated in October 1997 with the dedication of the Kansas Technology Center, the largest building project in Pittsburg State University history. The 260,000-square-foot facility covers a 20-acre site and cost nearly $30 million to complete. In 1995 the university received a $600,000 organ known as Fisk Opus 106. Dr. Susan Marchant of the Music Department presented the inaugural concert on the world-class instrument in McCray Hall auditorium.

On January 1, 1996, Dr. John Darling became the seventh president of Pittsburg State University. During Darling's tenure, a December commencement ceremony was added to the university calendar, Pittsburg State's chapter of Students in Free Enterprise was named international champion at the 1998 Students in Free Enterprise Exposition and Career Opportunity Fair, and renovations on historic Russ Hall began. Lesser renovations were also initiated or completed on Hughes, Yates, Whitesitt, and Willard halls, the John Lance arena, and the Horace Mann building. The promotion of educational technology, the addition of interactive classrooms, the introduction of online enrollment, an increase in study abroad opportunities, and the development of the Presidential Emerging Leadership program were also emphasized during the late 1990s. Darling retired from the presidency in early 1999 and the Board of Regents appointed Dr. Tom Bryant the eighth president of Pittsburg State a few months later, on July 1.

Change, advancement, and recognition continued as Pittsburg State approached its centennial year. In

Members of the ninth annual Paris summer program and European Study Tour in 1979. First row, left to right: Henri Freyburger, DeAnn Puckett, Pam Zimmerman, Josephine Marshall, Barbara Reed, Maxine Hackney, Henry Trabuc. Second row: Doretta Finnerty, Josephine Kinser, Dot Koehler, Janie Grimes. Third row: Brian West, Darcy Mendenhall, Rene Kevin Norris, Dee Spade. Fourth row: Ron Gariglietti, Gary Rader, Cathy Hale, Karen Rude.

2000 the university opened an outreach office in Overland Park, Kansas, called the Kansas City Metro Center, to offer area residents assistance in admission, academic programs, and alumni activities. In October 2001 the $9 million renovation of Russ Hall was finished, just two months after the completion of a $5.8 million renovation of Carnie Smith Stadium. In September 2002 a groundbreaking ceremony was held for the Pittsburg State University Veterans Memorial Amphitheater. It was dedicated on Memorial Day 2004 with Dole as the keynote speaker. The amphitheater features a half-size replica of the original Vietnam Memorial Wall, an oval reflecting pool, sculptures, seating for 275 visitors, and over 2,500 engraved granite memorial pavers that honor the service of U.S. veterans. The dedication of the Veterans Memorial was one of the final events in 2003 and 2004 to celebrate the university's first 100 years.

Students learned a variety of artistic techniques, including basket weaving, during a two-week workshop offered by the Art Department in July 1979. Other projects in the course consisted of tanning rabbit, sheep, and cow hides, and making paper from natural fibers.

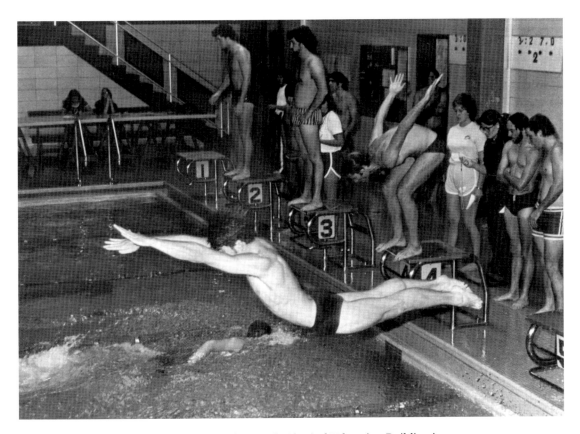

Intramural swimming relays were held in the Weede Physical Education Building in 1979.

The Iranian Student Association demonstrated against the shah and President Jimmy Carter on the Oval in 1979. More than twenty Iranian students had their enrollment canceled for nonpayment of fees when the mail service between Iran and the United States was disrupted, preventing them from receiving funds from Iran.

"Whatsa Gazebo?" T-shirts appeared on the campus prior to the seventy-fifth anniversary celebration on May 2, 1979. This group, pictured in front of the Student Union, includes many of the planners of the observance. Events included hot air balloon rides, a roasted buffalo dinner, and a gazebo with carnival-like entertainments.

Kansas governor John Carlin and Pittsburg State University President James Appleberry symbolically open the new university library following formal dedication ceremonies in October 1979. During a special ceremony in 1981, the new library was rededicated as the Leonard H. Axe Library, honoring the former college president.

Jeff Cooper, junior linebacker, and Timon Oujiri, senior offensive guard, undress after their 43–14 victory over the Peru (Nebraska) University Bobcats in the 1979 Boot Hill Bowl. Under coach Ron Randleman, the Gorillas ended the 1979 season with an 8–3 record.

Cadet Capt. Ervin Neff rappels off the Russ Hall roof as Sgt. Walter Martin belays him in 1980. ROTC was mandatory for male Pittsburg State students from 1952 until fall 1970, and military science has remained an attractive program for many university students. The rappelling exercise on Russ Hall in 1980 was a demonstration for high school students visiting the campus on Career Day.

John Pallett, university employee, tends the plants in the campus greenhouse in 1980.

F. Victor Sullivan, dean of technology from 1985 to 1995, constructed a Burt Rutan–designed VariEze tandem airplane in his living room in 1980. Rutan, an aeronautical engineer and former chief test pilot for the Air Force, said the fixed-wing fiberglass airplane had an estimated air speed of 160 miles per hour. From 1976 to 2005 the National Transportation Safety Board reported 130 accidents and 46 fatal accidents out of a fleet of 800 VariEze planes constructed nationwide.

Hugh Campbell, professor of biology, reviews his notes in 1980. Campbell and other science faculty were relocated to the Science Annex building after Carney Hall was closed in 1978. They remained in the temporary laboratory and classroom building until Heckert-Wells Hall opened in 1984.

Contestants speed across campus in a ten-mile bicycle race during the second annual Ape-Fest, in April 1981. For several years student organizations held Ape-Fest to re-create the atmosphere of the seventy-fifth Diamond Jubilee anniversary celebration. All proceeds from the carnival-type booths, concerts, and activities were to support the Alumni Association.

Gene DeGruson, curator of special collections at Pittsburg State University from 1963 to 1997, searches for information in response to a telephone inquiry in 1981. DeGruson, an acclaimed poet, historian, and thespian, was eulogized as a southeast Kansas treasure when he passed away in June 1997.

Jackie Allen (left) listens to the keynote speaker at Apple Day ceremonies in March 1981. The speaker, Bernard Franklin, chairman of the Board of Regents, kept the Pittsburg State faculty on the edge of their seats as he discussed faculty salaries.

Apple Day button from March 2, 1977.

"Easy Riders" in 1981. Mopeds came into vogue during the energy crisis of the late 1970s. Professors (left to right) David Vequist, Richard Jacques, David Butler, and Robert Roberts from the Department of Printing all rode mopeds between school and home.

Alireza Adibi enjoys the Student Union game room in 1982. Pinball and other traditional games came under pressure, however, from the growing popularity of Atari and other video games in the early 1980s.

Local members of the Society for Creative Anachronism re-created the Middle Ages on campus in 1983. Tournaments and other events provided an opportunity to learn about martial arts during the Middle Ages and the peaceful arts of calligraphy, dancing, and needleworking.

James Potts uses a skateboard as an alternate form of transportation on campus in September 1981.

Chris Lake relaxes in his dorm room with his extensive music collection in 1984.

A party held in Gibson Dining Hall encouraged students to vote in the 1984 national elections. The Crawford County Clerk's Office reported that over 1,500 students on campus, more than 30 percent of the student population, registered to vote at the event. A heavy voter turnout on campus and across the nation secured the reelection of President Ronald Reagan and his vice president, George H. W. Bush.

After five weeks of rehearsals, Pittsburg student Lora McMurray (front) and members of the university cast presented *West Side Story* in 1985. A new twist was added to the classic play because the Jets and the Sharks were punk gangs. John Green, an exchange faculty member from England, directed the play.

President Donald Wilson boosts the spirits of the crowd at his first homecoming convocation in October 1984. Wilson became the sixth president of Pittsburg State University in December 1983.

LEFT: Internationally known sex therapist Dr. Ruth Westheimer came to Pittsburg as a guest lecturer in the fall of 1985. Her talk on sex education was profiled on the popular CBS television show *60 Minutes* in January 1986, and the footage included questions from members of the Pittsburg audience.

BELOW: Dedication ceremonies for the Francis A. Monahan Outdoor Education Center were held in October 1988. The 156-acre education center, located six miles southwest of the university campus, was donated by Norma Monahan Reals and her husband, Dr. William Reals. The property is managed jointly by the Pittsburg State Biology Department and the Crawford County Conservation Department.

Staci Antill and Johnny Warrick were selected to portray Gussie and Gus in the fall of 1988. Gussie first appeared on campus in 1980 as part of an increasing interest in women's athletics, and she lasted until the women's teams became known as the Lady Gorillas in the fall of 1989.

Alpha Phi Alpha fraternity members perform a step show for local schoolchildren in 1989.

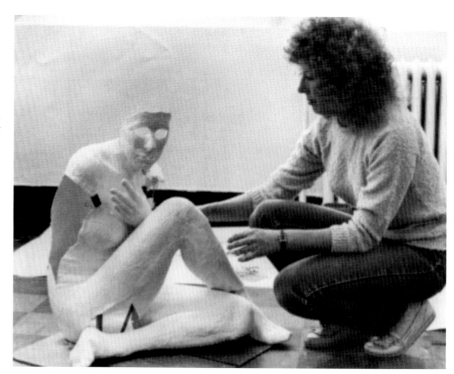

Teresa McBee works on a plaster of Paris sculpture of herself during a session of the Designed World Art class in 1989.

The International Bazaar in 1989 featured the touring Dancers and Musicians of Bali. The Balinese orchestra, Gamelan Gong Kebyar, provided accompaniment for the dancers, who portrayed the story of Naten Dirah and her female entourage, who were all students of black magic.

August Rua, an alumnus of the Kansas State Teachers College of Pittsburg, entered the insurance business after graduating in 1955. He was co-founder and president of the Alumni Foundation and served as a member of the alumni board of directors. August and Helen Rua donated funds for major renovations to the football stadium and field between 1986 and 1989. In September 1989 the university's new press box in Carnie Smith Stadium was dedicated as the August and Helen Rua Press Box.

More than 500 students, administrators and instructors, and community members gathered at a rally in the Overman Student Center in January 1991 to show support for the American soldiers involved in Operation Desert Storm. After the rally Col. Jim AuBuchon, then director of career services at Pittsburg State University, said, "In recent times, people have said this generation of students is more concerned about themselves than others. What we saw here today in support of the troops flies in the face of that."

A student in the Geography Department examines a lump of coal. Bituminous coal deposits in Crawford and Cherokee counties led to the establishment of the city of Pittsburg in 1876 and prompted thousands of European immigrants to come to work in the region's deep-shaft mines.

Desk graffiti in 1992.

Pete Hamilton, known for many years as the "voice of the Gorillas," reads off track and field results in 1992. Hamilton's trademark expression at home football games—"welcome to the jungle"—has endeared him to generations of Gorilla fans.

Gary Green, a 1974 graduate, returned to Pittsburg from New York City to act as master of ceremonies in a Pittsburg State production of *Cabaret* in 1992.

The nondenominational Timmons Chapel celebrated twenty-five years of services and programs in 1991. On October 2, 1966, a Catholic priest, a Protestant minister, and a rabbi dedicated the chapel, which was a gift to the university from Bess Timmons. The chapel was constructed in a Country English Gothic style of architecture with native limestone walls and a Vermont slate roof. Inside the chapel, hand-carved solid oak doors and stained-glass windows accent the sanctuary.

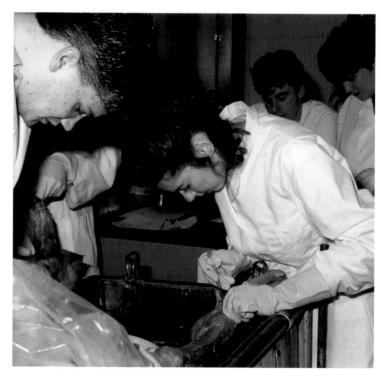

Anatomy students (from left) Shawn Bowman, Jennifer Clayton, Shawn Jordan, and Julie Brown study cadavers obtained by Pittsburg State University from the Willed Body Program operated by the University of Kansas Medical Center in 1993.

Gus the Gorilla, President John Darling, and Student Government Association President Alison Auxter cut the ribbon at the Gorilla Village opening on September 26, 1998. Gorilla Village, next to the stadium and the University Lake, is the venue for many university activities, including GorillaFest before each home football game.

President Tom Bryant addresses the audience during the March 2000 Apple Day Convocation in McCray Hall Auditorium. Bryant had become the eighth president of Pittsburg State University the previous July.

Matt Campbell, a member of the Gorillahead Rugby Club, takes the pitch during a contest in 2002. Though not a varsity sport, the club competes in at least twenty games a year and participates in the Heart of America Union, which includes college and university teams from Kansas and Missouri.

The Pride of the Plains Marching Band entertains at a home football game in 2004.

Kansas Senator Robert Dole addresses the audience at the dedication of the Kansas Technology Center in October 1997. Dole was instrumental in obtaining $9 million in federal funding for the center. On May 31, 2004, a wing of the building was rededicated as the Senator Robert J. Dole Technology Building.

Participants in the dedication ceremony for the Kansas Technology Center gather in the F. Victor Sullivan Courtyard on October 24, 1997. The courtyard was named for Sullivan, dean of technology and applied science, who was instrumental in the planning and fund-raising that led to the construction of the center.

A popular spot of beauty on the campus is the University Lake. In 1934 a group of Civil Works Administration workers began transforming the former farm pond by landscaping and terracing the surrounding grounds and building a gravel walkway encircling the lake. In 1958 local conservationist W. J. "Red" Fox significantly expanded the lake's length and depth and created the island in the center. In recent years two fountains and a waterfall on the north end of the lake were added.

Chapter Nine

THE CENTENNIAL CELEBRATION

This school started out as the impossible dream of R. S. Russ, but it nevertheless came into being to produce some of the best alumni of any institution in the world, and it will continue to dream—and do.

Gene DeGruson

THE FIRST DAY of classes at Pittsburg State University was September 8, 1903. On September 8, 2003, the university hosted a centennial birthday celebration called the PittNic for the campus and Pittsburg community. Several thousand people attended the celebration held on the university Oval. They witnessed Jennifer Waugh, an undergraduate from Cherokee, Kansas, take home the grand prize of a Ford F-150 Harley-Davidson edition truck. Ten other students won Lee and Linda Scott Centennial Scholarships worth $2,500 each.

The earliest centennial events were held during the spring 2003 semester. A Centennial Gala initiated the festivities and raised nearly $20,000 for the general scholarship fund. A celebration in the rotunda of the state capitol in Topeka paid tribute to the Kansas legislature's action that established the normal school in Pittsburg. Apple Day in March 2003 included remarks by alumnus Harlan Hess, who spoke of his football career and continual pride in his alma mater. The first annual Gorilla Century bicycle ride was held in the summer of 2003 with more than 170 riders from the four-state region of Kansas, Missouri, Oklahoma, and Arkansas participating in the 100-mile event. In the fall

of 2003, a centennial symposium brought international alumni and representatives of partner universities from around the world to the Pittsburg campus. During a special ceremony in September 2003, the university honored H. Lee Scott Jr., president and CEO of Wal-Mart and a 1971 Pittsburg State graduate. Scott presented the inaugural William A. Brandenburg Lecture and received the first Brandenburg Award, named for president of Pittsburg State University.

Commemoration Day in March 2004 featured Governor Kathleen Sebelius as the keynote speaker. Every graduate who donned a cap and gown in May 2003, December 2003, and May 2004 received a specially cast commemorative centennial medallion. The celebration also produced several lasting visual tributes to the first 100 years of Pittsburg State University history, including an official Pittsburg State ring designed by students, alumni, and staff and a centennial mural, in which Pittsburg State graduate Mark Switlik conceived and painted twenty-one distinct images on the north end of Nation Hall that reflect important aspects of the university's rich history.

Although the centennial tribute celebrated the university's history, it also celebrated community and rec-

STATE OF KANSAS

PROCLAMATION BY THE GOVERNOR

TO THE PEOPLE OF KANSAS, GREETINGS:

WHEREAS, on Feb. 21, 1903, Kansas Governor Willis J. Bailey signed Senate Bill 234 that established a Manual Training Normal School in Pittsburg as an auxiliary to the Normal School in Emporia; and the institution opened its doors with 54 students in 1903, with the purpose to prepare teachers of the industrial and domestic arts; and

WHEREAS, Pittsburg State University now offers more than 100 outstanding undergraduate and graduate programs in the Arts and Sciences, Education, Business and Technology; and today has more than 6,750 students with 97 percent of those taking classes on the campus in Pittsburg; and

WHEREAS, Pittsburg State University is accredited by the North Central Association of Colleges and Secondary Schools, and has many individual academic programs that have earned prestigious accreditation from state and national organizations; and

WHEREAS, Pittsburg State University intercollegiate athletic teams, the Gorillas, have earned regional and national recognition for their accomplishments in both academic and athletic competition; and

WHEREAS, Pittsburg State University serves as a cultural center, provides significant support for economic development activities, and is involved in numerous activities for Kansas and;

WHEREAS, Pittsburg State University has more than 22,000 alumni living in the state of Kansas and more than 50,000 worldwide who contribute to the betterment of society in many significant ways; and

WHEREAS, Pittsburg State University is joining with its many constituents to celebrate its Centennial and pay tribute to the University's rich legacy.

NOW THEREFORE, I, KATHLEEN SEBELIUS, GOVERNOR OF THE STATE OF KANSAS, do hereby proclaim Wednesday, February 19, 2003 as

Pittsburg State University Centennial Celebration Day

in Kansas in recognition of this university's 100 years of outstanding service to higher education and the people of Kansas.

DONE: At the Capitol in Topeka under the Great Seal of the State this 14th day of February, A.D. 2003

BY THE GOVERNOR: _____

_____
Secretary of State

_____
Assistant Secretary of State

On February 14, 2003, Governor Kathleen Sebelius signed a special proclamation declaring Wednesday, February 19, 2003, as Pittsburg State University Centennial Celebration Day.

Governor Kathleen Sebelius greets President Tom Bryant and shakes hands with Gus Gorilla moments before a celebration in the state Capitol rotunda.

ognized people who had dedicated their lives to the institution's success. In 1983 historian Robert Ratzlaff documented well over 200 people who had spent at least twenty years at the university. Approximately fifty faculty members, Ratzlaff wrote, "spent at least 30 years at this institution. Several were here more than 40 years, including Ernest Baxter and Otto Hankammer in Industrial Arts, Rose Buchman, Gabriella Campbell, and Marjorie Jackson in Music, John Lance and Garfield Weede in Physical Education, Odella Nation in the Library, and J. Ralph Wells in Biology." He continued, "Very few institutions of higher learning the size of Pittsburg State could cite similar statistics." That tradition continues, as evidenced most

recently by James Schick in History, Ken Gordon in Automotive Technology, Stephen Teller in English, Marjorie Schick in Art, Warren Deatherage in Education, and Vice President Robert Ratzlaff.

Another underlying theme during the celebration of Pittsburg State's first 100 years was a re-emphasis of the university's commitment to its students and alumni. During the centennial celebration the university community openly adopted and promoted the belief "once a Gorilla, always a Gorilla." As thoughts turned to a second century, those committed to the university's future agreed that in the foreseeable future and beyond it would continue to be a place where people succeed.

Pittsburg State friends of all ages attended the centennial "PittNic," held on the campus Oval September 8, 2003, to commemorate the 100th anniversary of the first day of classes at the Kansas State Manual Training Normal School Auxiliary.

Kenny McDougle, professor of curriculum and instruction, participates in the first annual Gorilla Century bicycle ride in August 2003. Riders from the four-state region followed marked courses of 30, 60, or 100 miles through the countryside around Pittsburg.

A centennial medallion was specially cast to honor Pittsburg State graduates. All graduates, faculty, and administrators who donned the cap and gown in May 2003, December 2003, and May 2004 received one of the medallions.

The Centennial Bell Tower rises above Yates Hall, and a portion of the Leonard H. Axe Library looms in the background. The brick pedestal and bronze plaques (lower left) mark the site of the original campus gymnasium, which was razed in 1972. On May 14, 2004, the university placed a time capsule below the foundation of the bell tower. Centennial memorabilia, university publications, and recordings were among the thirty-one items selected for placement in the capsule.

Thousands attended the centennial PittNic, where full-time enrolled students were registered for the grand prize drawing of a new Ford truck and for ten scholarships worth $2,500 each.

The winner of the banana-eating contest during the centennial festivities receives the congratulations and adulation of fellow students.

The luckiest student at the centennial PittNic was Jennifer Waugh, an undergraduate from Cherokee, Kansas. Waugh won the drawing for a grand prize of a Ford F-150 Harley-Davidson edition truck. The Midwest Ford Dealers Association donated the special edition truck to honor the 2003 centennials of the university, the Ford Motor Company, and the Harley-Davidson Corporation.

University employees and Sodexho Food Service chefs oversaw preparation and service for the thousands attending the centennial PittNic.

Hundreds who attended the PittNic pose for the official centennial portrait, taken just before the birthday cake was served. Mascot Gus Gorilla is flanked by President Tom Bryant and Koeta Bryant.

President Tom Bryant and first lady Koeta Bryant were joined by student leaders, retired faculty, and university staff to serve the centennial birthday cake to the thousands who attended the PittNic the evening of September 8, 2003.

Alumni and friends of Pittsburg State University frequently gathered in Gorilla Village for centennial events.

The founders of Pittsburg State University knew they faced a tall order trying to establish a new school in 1903. Little could they have imagined all the worthy accomplishments of the university in its first 100 years.

Professor emeritus Charlene Lingo of the Department of Special Services and Leadership Studies was in the 1903 spirit during the 2003 PittNic celebration.

H. Lee Scott Jr., president and CEO of Wal-Mart, visits with President Tom Bryant in McCray Auditorium just before delivering the inaugural William A. Brandenburg Lecture in September 2003.

Chapter Ten

AFTERWORD:
SINCE THE CENTENNIAL, 2004–2008

Research, Instruction, Service

Pittsburg State University seal

As the celebration of the Pittsburg State University centennial came to a close in early 2004, it was an appropriate time to reflect upon a proud past and to contemplate what the future held for the institution. Rising tuition costs and fewer federal and state dollars for higher education would be only two of the challenges facing the university in its second century. Yet, in the five years following 2004, the university experienced growth in enrollments, the addition of several new facilities, adapted to the retirement of several key leaders, received major gifts and allocations, and garnered national and international recognition for its accomplishments and the contributions of its faculty and alumni.

In the spring 2007 semester, Pittsburg State University set a record with 6,422 on-campus students enrolled, only to see that number eclipsed in the fall 2007 semester when, for the first time in its history, the university's enrollment surpassed 7,000. As student numbers increased, so did the size of the campus. In September 2007, Kansas Governor Kathleen Sebelius participated in the opening of the state-of-the-art Tyler Research Center building—the new home of the Kansas Polymer Research Center. A new $15 million

combination student recreation center, National Guard Armory, and classroom building was dedicated in 2008, and the construction of a new student health center began in the fall of 2008.

The university paid special recognition in 2006 to the retirements of Dr. James AuBuchon and Dr. Robert Ratzlaff, who were among the many outstanding long-time members of the faculty and staff who have retired since the centennial year. AuBuchon, a 1963 graduate, returned to the campus in August 1967 after a tour of active duty with the U.S. Army to become a career administrator in student affairs while continuing his connections with the military. In 1999 he retired from the army with the rank of brigadier general after thirty-six years of active and reserve duty. One year earlier, in 1998, AuBuchon was named vice president for university advancement and executive director of the Pittsburg State University Foundation, Inc. Ratzlaff began his career at the university as a history professor in 1966. He was chairman of the History Department from 1978 to 1986, then served the university for twenty years as vice president of academic affairs.

In January 2008 the Kansas Technology Center received more than $260,000 for updates to technol-

The Galloping Horse of Gansu was installed at the University Lake in May 2003. It was a gift of Huo Baozhu, president of the Shaanxi Five Rings Sculptural Art Company. The sculpture is a replica of the original *Galloping Horse,* circa AD 25–100, unearthed in 1969 in the excavation of an East Han Dynasty tomb in China.

ogy and equipment. At the same time, the Caterpillar and Martin Tractor Company made additional gifts of heavy equipment to the Technology Center, bringing the total of recent gifts to nearly $1 million. The Kansas Polymer Research Center received approximately $1.1 million from the 2008 Federal Omnibus Bill, and private donations of nearly $1.7 million allowed for additional updates to the football stadium and the installation of a new video screen display in the fall of 2008.

The accolades for Pittsburg State students, faculty, and alumni have been numerous in recent years. In 2006 a team of students designed, built, and raced the winning vehicle in the annual NASA Great Moon-buggy Race in Huntsville, Alabama, while a second

group of Pittsburg students designed an experiment that was selected to go on a NASA zero-gravity research plane. In January 2008 nearly fifty choir members and Music Department faculty traveled to Germany to perform concerts in Heidelberg and Munich. And in 2007 Arnoldsche Art Publishers of Stuttegart, Germany, published *Sculpture to Wear: The Jewelry of Marjorie Schick.* Schick, a professor in the Department of Art, has earned an international reputation for her work and is one of 200 artists to be named a Fellow of the American Crafts Council.

The Association of International Educators honored the university with its 2008 Senator Paul Simon Award for Campus Internationalization. Pittsburg State was one of four colleges and universities nation-

Robert D. Tyler, a Pittsburg graduate in 1975 and the founder of Winfield Consumer Products, was the major donor for the construction of the new Tyler Research Center. The first phase of the center, dedicated in September 2007, contains twenty-one laboratories and nine offices used by the Kansas Polymer Research Center, which has worked with Cargill Inc. for more than a decade to make from vegetable and soybean oils such products traditionally made with petroleum as foam and resin. These efforts were rewarded in 2007 with the Presidential Green Chemistry Challenge Award, making it the only research institution in Kansas to win the prize.

wide to receive this award, which recognizes outstanding and innovative efforts in campus internationalization. Pittsburg alumni in the spotlight recently have included Gene Bicknell, a 1953 graduate and the founder of NPC International. James Press, a 1968 graduate, has been featured in a variety of national publications in recent months after becoming president of Toyota Motor Sales USA, the first non-Japanese person to hold the position with Toyota. H. Lee Scott, the CEO of Wal-Mart and a 1971 gradu-

ate, has also garnered international attention while directing the activities of the world's largest corporation.

Preparation, success, and advancement are ideals that are a part of the fabric of Pittsburg State University. There will always be challenges that conspire against the university's ideals and goals, but together the administration, faculty, staff, students, alumni, and friends of the university will endeavor to make its second century even greater.

The Student Recreation Center/National Guard Armory is a unique cooperative effort between the university and the Kansas Army National Guard. The building houses four gymnasiums, a wide array of fitness equipment, and areas for study and entertainment. It also serves as home to the Department of Military Science and the Department of Health, Human Performance and Recreation.

The student body passed a health center referendum vote in April 2008, and construction of the new student health center began the next fall. The new facility will serve the student population as a center for both physical and mental health.

Renowned White House correspondent and former White House bureau chief for United Press International Helen Thomas was the keynote speaker for the 2007 edition of the annual university lecture series, "Profiles of Women in Government." Thomas, named one of the twenty-five most influential women in America, served with United Press International for fifty-seven years and traveled around the world with presidents Richard Nixon, Gerald Ford, Jimmy Carter, Ronald Reagan, George H. W. Bush, Bill Clinton, and George W. Bush. At the lecture, Thomas received a standing ovation and lengthy applause following her comments on the topics of women in politics, the Iraq war, and the presidents she covered as a correspondent.

Night Song is a bronze statue of a Plains Indian playing a courting flute. The statue was designed and executed by Joe Beeler, a 1957 graduate of the college and a renowned western artist.

Judith Shaw, professor of history, was honored in 2008 for her long tenure as a member of the Pittsburg faculty. Though it has been common for members of the Pittsburg faculty and classified staff to complete twenty, thirty, or even forty years at Pittsburg State, Shaw is making history as she begins her fiftieth year as a member of the university faculty. The longest previous tenure at the university was held by the original faculty member, Odella Nation, who served from 1903 to 1951.

No matter their age,
Pittsburg State University supporters
ensure a bright future for the institution.

References

___

PAGE 2: Porter quotation: "Is Now a Law," *Pittsburg Daily Headlight*, February 21, 1903, 3; PAGE 2: Wheeler to Cliggitt, February 19, 1903, Morris Cliggitt Papers, Leonard H. Axe Library, Pittsburg State University; PAGE 3: "To Beautify Pittsburg," ibid., February 24, 1903, 4; PAGES 14–15: Russ quotation: "Farewell to Russ," *Manual Normal Light*, June 1911, 12; PAGE 15: Myers quotation: "The Inauguration," ibid., December 1911, 1–2; PAGE 17: "*The Mikado*," ibid. [*Mikado* Edition], March 1911, 154; PAGE 23: William Bawden, *A History of Kansas State Teachers College, 1903–1941*, (Pittsburg: Kansas State Teachers College, 1952), 99; PAGE 32: *Kanza* (Pittsburg: State Manual Training Normal, 1920), 147; PAGE 40: "Sittin' in a Corner" lyrics: ibid., 1924, 194; PAGE 41: Pep club quotation: ibid., 1942, 134–135; ibid., 1943, 72; PAGES 59–61: Ratzlaff quotation: Robert K. Ratzlaff, "A Brief History of Pittsburg State University," *Bulletin of Pittsburg State University Graduate Studies*, December 1983, 13; PAGE 62: Russ Hall description: *Collegio*, March 22, 1935, 1; PAGE 62: Pitkin quotation: ibid., June 7, 1935, 1; PAGE 62: Brandenburg quotation: ibid., June 7, 1935, 1; PAGE 65: Weiss quotation: ibid., October 1, 1947, 2; PAGE 114: Russ quotation: ibid., August 28, 1962, 1; PAGE 115: Dress code description: *Kansas State College of Pittsburg Student Handbook, 1963–1964* (Pittsburg: Kansas State College of Pittsburg, 1963), 57; PAGE 116: Budd quotation: *Alumnian* (Kansas State College of Pittsburg), Summer 1975, 3; PAGE 139: Nevins quotation: Irma Gene Nevins, "Brandenburg Vision and Leadership Have Influenced Growth of College," *Collegio Anniversary Supplement*, March 18, 1938, 8; PAGE 177: *Collegio*, January 29, 1991, 1; PAGE 187: Ratzlaff quotation: Ratzlaff, "Brief History of Pittsburg State University," 11.

Wild Horse Creek and *Autumn Symphony,* two oil paintings by Birger Sandzen, were acquired by the college in 1945. Sandzen, a native of Sweden, became one of Kansas's best-known landscape artists. He taught art at Bethany College in Lindsborg, Kansas, for many years and exhibited many of his works on the Pittsburg campus during the 1930s and 1940s.

Index